Gourmet every Day

from the editors of Gourmet

Photographs by Romulo A. Yanes

Condé Nast Books   Random House

New York

Copyright © 2000
The Condé Nast Publications Inc. All rights
reserved under International and Pan-
American Copyright Conventions. Published
in the United States by Random House, Inc.,
New York, and simultaneously in Canada by
Random House of Canada Limited, Toronto.

LIBRARY OF CONGRESS
CATALOGING-IN-PUBLICATION DATA
GOURMET EVERY DAY/from the editors of *Gourmet*
    p. cm.
    Includes index.
    ISBN 0-375-50445-1
    1. Quick and easy cookery. 2. Dinners and
dining. I. Gourmet

TX833.5 .G68 2000
641.5'52—dc21   00-035319

Random House website address:
www.atrandom.com

Some of the recipes in this work were
published previously in *Gourmet* magazine.

Printed in the United States of America
on acid-free paper.

98765432
First Edition

Informative text was written by Diane Keitt,
Ellen Morrissey, Jane Daniels Lear, and
Zanne Stewart.

Front Jacket: Warm Pasta Salad with Baby
Spinach and Tuna (page 55).
Back Jacket: Seared Salmon with Sesame-
Spinach Bok Choy (page 68).

FOR CONDÉ NAST BOOKS
Lisa Faith Phillips, *Vice President/
    General Manager*
Tom Downing, *Direct Marketing Director*
Deborah Williams, *Operations Manager*
Colleen P. Shire, *Direct Marketing Manager*
Angela Lee, *Assistant Direct Marketing Manager*
Meredith Peters, *Direct Marketing Associate*
Richard B. Elman, *Production Manager*

FOR GOURMET BOOKS
Diane Keitt, *Director*
Ellen Morrissey, *Associate Editor*

FOR GOURMET MAGAZINE
Ruth Reichl, *Editor-in-Chief*

Zanne Early Stewart, *Executive Food Editor*
Kemp Miles Minifie, *Senior Food Editor*
Alexis M. Touchet, *Associate Food Editor*
Lori Walther Powell, *Food Editor*
Elizabeth Vought, *Food Editor*
Katy Massam, *Food Editor*
Shelton Wiseman, *Food Editor*
Ruth Cousineau, *Food Editor*

Romulo A. Yanes, *Photographer*
Marjorie H. Webb, *Style Director*
Nancy Purdum, *Senior Style Editor*

Produced in association with
MEDIA PROJECTS INCORPORATED
Carter Smith, *Executive Editor*
Anne B. Wright, *Project Editor*
John W. Kern, *Production Consultant*
Aaron R. Murray, *Production Editor*
Marilyn Flaig, *Indexer*

Salsgiver Coveney Associates, Inc.
Jacket and Book Design

The text of this book was set in Filosofia by
Media Projects Incorporated. The four-color
separations were done by American Color,
Applied Graphic Technologies, and
Quad/Graphics, Inc. The book was printed and
bound at R. R. Donnelley and Sons. Stock is
Citation Web Gloss, Westvāco.

acknowledgments

In keeping with the "quick" nature of this cookbook, recipes were created on a very tight schedule. We would like to thank *Gourmet*'s food editors: Alexis Touchet (grills and grains); Lori Powell (vegetables, sandwiches, and snacks, as well as the salmon recipe on the back jacket); Liz Vought (soups and salads); Shelley Wiseman (stove-tops and desserts); Ruth Cousineau (pastas and pizzas, including the pasta recipe on the front jacket); and Tasha Garcia, who cross-tested many of these recipes. Zanne Stewart, Executive Food Editor, and Kemp Minifie, Senior Food Editor, acted as tasters and consultants; and Gerald Asher, *Gourmet*'s Wine Editor, chose wines to accompany the menus.

Romulo Yanes, *Gourmet*'s photographer, along with prop stylist Susan Victoria, food stylist Liz Vought, and hand model Colleen Shire, captured the essence of simplicity for our jacket. Throughout the book are color images by Romulo that have been prop-styled by Marjorie Webb and Nancy Purdum. Additional photographs were contributed by Alan Richardson, Quentin Bacon, and Ellen Silverman.

Many informational boxes were written by our colleagues, Zanne Stewart, Jane Daniels Lear, and Alexis Touchet. Anne Wright, Aaron Murray, and John Kern handled all production matters, while Cheryl Brown and Kathleen Duffy Freud kept an editorial eye. Finally, thanks to Karen Salsgiver, master of color and space, for a big, bright, beautiful design.

The Editors of Gourmet Books

CONTENTS

Introduction by *Ruth Reichl* 11

one-DISH DINNERS 12

salads for dinner 32

QUICK

CONTENTS

1   Stove-top Dishes 56

2   Grills 76

3   Soups 90

4   Sandwiches and Burgers 102

5   Pastas and Pizzas 116

6   Vegetables 134

7   Grains 146

8   Green Salads 154

9   Snacks 168

10   Desserts 176

Index of Recipes 191

Table Setting
Acknowledgments 203

Credits 206

INTRODUCTION

Everybody who works at *Gourmet* magazine loves to cook. Otherwise we wouldn't be here. But last year we sat down to a candid discussion, and once we stopped bragging about the fabulous feasts with which we dazzle our friends on the weekends, we faced the honest truth: Weeknights are a different story. Most nights we work late and go home to hungry families who don't want to wait while we concoct some magnificent creation. They want dinner. They want it fast. And they want it to be delicious. And, if we are going to be entirely truthful, after a hard day at the office, simplicity is extremely appealing. Even if you're addicted to cooking, there are times when you're tempted to order out.

And so *Gourmet Every Day* was born. The challenge was to create recipes so delicious—and so easy—that cooking would be a breeze for even the most exhausted homemaker. We knew it was a good idea, but we did not anticipate that it would soon become the most cherished section of the magazine.

These are the recipes that we all use, constantly. They're the ones that we sneak home before they're even printed, the recipes our families repeatedly request. And frankly, they're the hardest to invent. With the luxuries of time, money, and calories, it is not all that difficult to come up with wonderful recipes. But each time you add another restriction, the task becomes more difficult. Especially when your standards are high.

Creating quick and easy recipes without sacrificing flavor is quite a challenge. You see, to qualify for *Gourmet Every Day*, a recipe must be more than fast. It must not rely on convenience foods. It must occasionally be low calorie. But above all it must be truly tasty.

We are very proud of the recipes we have created for *Gourmet Every Day*, including the 100 new ones developed for this book. In all, 200 recipes appear here, and none takes more than 45 minutes. The many that can be made in 20 minutes or less are marked with a lightning bolt ⚡ . And because so many of us prefer eating lightly during the week, we've designed 50 of these recipes for the fat and calorie conscious. They're marked with a feather 🪶 and they have all the significant numbers appended to the bottom.

You'll find recipes for everything from snacks to desserts, but the heart of the book is the one-dish meals. I'm particularly partial to the shrimp and corn with basil; it takes only 20 minutes, and it's fancy enough for a party. That warm pasta salad with baby spinach and tuna is another big favorite, as is the lean, light saffron chicken and chickpea stew.

These are all terrific dishes. But they are more than mere recipes: They are proof that you can work all day and still go home and cook a great meal.

Ruth Reichl
Editor-in-Chief

one-DISH

dinners

To coax you into your apron after a long hard day, we've created a collection of fabulous single recipes that serve as delicious dinners. On every left-hand page is a full-color photograph of a meal-in-one; on the right is the corresponding recipe (with everyday wine selections, too). Dinner will be ready in 45 minutes or less. While efficiency is key, we encourage you to relax and have a sip of that suggested wine. Just don't forget to preheat the oven, if you're using it. And, as every pro knows, it always saves time to prep and assemble ingredients before you start to cook.

ROASTED CHICKEN LEGS WITH VEGETABLES AND ARUGULA

Serves 2

2   whole chicken legs (1 lb), cut into
     thighs and drumsticks
¾   lb small boiling potatoes, halved
1   red bell pepper, cut into ½-inch-wide strips
1   medium onion, cut into ½-inch-thick wedges
1   tablespoon olive oil
½   teaspoon dried thyme, crumbled
1   bunch arugula (2 cups), coarse stems discarded
¼   cup dry white wine

Preheat oven to 450°F.

Pat chicken dry. Toss chicken, potatoes, bell pepper, and onion with oil, thyme, and salt and pepper to taste in a large flameproof roasting pan until coated and arrange in 1 layer, chicken skin sides up. Roast 30 minutes, or until chicken is cooked through and golden.

Put arugula in a large bowl and add chicken and vegetables, transferring with tongs. Add wine to pan and deglaze over moderately high heat, stirring and scraping up brown bits, 1 minute. Pour sauce over chicken and vegetables and toss. Recipe may be doubled to serve 4.

 Benziger Sonoma County Merlot 1997

ROASTED MUSSELS WITH ALMONDS AND GARLIC

Serves 2

$2\frac{1}{2}$ lb mussels (preferably cultivated), cleaned and beards removed

4   garlic cloves, minced

$\frac{1}{2}$ cup fresh flat-leaf parsley, chopped

$\frac{3}{4}$ cup dry white wine

3   tablespoons unsalted butter

$\frac{1}{4}$ cup natural whole almonds, finely chopped and toasted

ACCOMPANIMENTS:
crusty bread and green salad

Preheat oven to 425° F.

Combine mussels, garlic, parsley, wine, and butter in an ovenproof pot (at least 10 inches wide) and season with pepper. Roast mussels, uncovered, in middle of oven, stirring once halfway through roasting, 15 minutes, or until mussels have opened. (Discard any unopened mussels.) Add almonds, tossing to combine.

 Crozes-Hermitage Blanc, Les Launes, Delas Frères 1997

GRILLED RIB-EYE STEAKS ON SAUTÉED ONIONS AND GARLIC CROÛTES WITH CURRY OIL

Serves 2

2   tablespoons olive oil
2   large onions, thinly sliced
2   (1-inch-thick) boneless rib-eye steaks (6 oz each)
½   teaspoon curry powder
2   (½-inch-thick) slices country-style bread
1   garlic clove, halved lengthwise

ACCOMPANIMENT:
green salad

Heat 1 tablespoon olive oil in a large heavy skillet over moderate heat until hot but not smoking, then cook onions with salt and pepper to taste, stirring, 15 minutes, or until golden brown. Keep warm, covered.

Pat steaks dry and season with salt and pepper. Heat an oiled well-seasoned ridged grill pan over moderately high heat until hot but not smoking, then grill steaks 3 to 4 minutes on each side for medium-rare.

While steaks are grilling, stir together curry powder and remaining tablespoon oil in a small saucepan and heat over moderate heat until hot but not smoking. Remove from heat and season curry oil with salt. Transfer steaks to a plate and let stand 5 minutes.

Toast bread and rub 1 side of hot toasts with cut sides of garlic. Top each *croûte* with onions and steak. Spoon curry oil (being careful not to include powder that has settled to bottom) over and around steaks.

 Meridian Vineyards Paso Robles Syrah 1997

SHRIMP AND FENNEL RISOTTO

Serves 2 generously

6   oz medium shrimp (12 to 15), peeled, deveined,
    and halved lengthwise
1   large fennel bulb (sometimes called anise),
    including fronds if possible
1   cup chicken broth
3   cups water
1   small onion, finely chopped
1   tablespoon unsalted butter
⅔   cup Arborio rice
¼   cup dry white wine

Put shrimp in a bowl and season with salt. Trim fennel stalks
flush with bulb, reserving fronds and discarding stalks, and trim
any discolored outer layers. Halve bulb lengthwise and discard
core. Finely chop bulb. Finely chop enough reserved fronds to
measure about 2 tablespoons. Bring broth and water to a simmer
in a 1½-quart saucepan and keep at a bare simmer.

Cook onion and fennel bulb in butter in a 2-quart heavy
saucepan over moderately low heat, stirring, until softened. Add
rice and cook, stirring, 2 minutes. Increase heat to moderate and
add wine. Cook, stirring, 1 minute. Stir in ½ cup simmering
broth and cook, stirring constantly and keeping at a strong simmer, until broth is absorbed. Continue cooking and adding broth,
½ cup at a time, stirring constantly and letting each addition be
absorbed before adding next, until rice is tender and creamy-
looking but still al dente, 18 to 20 minutes total. (There will be
broth left over.)

Stir shrimp into risotto and cook, stirring constantly, until
shrimp are just cooked through, about 3 minutes. If desired, thin
risotto to desired consistency with some leftover broth. Stir in
fennel fronds and salt and pepper to taste and serve immediately.

 Château de Rully, Rully Blanc 1998

CORNED BEEF HASH
Serves 4

- 1 lb baking (russet) potatoes, peeled and cut into ¼-inch dice
- 1 (1-lb) piece cooked corned beef, cut into chunks
- 1 cup chopped onion
- 1 large red bell pepper, cut into ¼-inch pieces
- 2 tablespoons unsalted butter
- ¼ cup heavy cream
- 4 large eggs (optional)
- 1 tablespoon chopped fresh flat-leaf parsley

ACCOMPANIMENT:
green salad

Cook potatoes in boiling salted water to cover until just tender, about 3 minutes, then drain. Pulse corned beef in a food processor until coarsely chopped.

Sauté onion and bell pepper in butter in a 12-inch nonstick skillet over moderately high heat, stirring, until lightly browned, about 5 minutes. Add potatoes and sauté over moderately high heat, stirring occasionally, until browned, about 5 minutes. Stir in corned beef and salt and pepper to taste, then cook, stirring occasionally, until browned. Add cream and cook, stirring, 1 minute.

If desired, make 4 holes in hash and break 1 egg into each. Cook over moderately low heat, covered, 5 minutes, or until eggs are cooked to desired doneness, and season with salt and pepper. Sprinkle hash with parsley.

 Tria Dry Creek Zinfandel 1997

SALMON KEDGEREE

Serves 2

1¾   cups water
½   teaspoon salt
1   (8-oz) piece skinned salmon fillet
¾   cup long-grain white rice
1   small onion, coarsely chopped
1   tablespoon unsalted butter
2   large hard-boiled eggs, peeled and quartered
2   tablespoons chopped fresh flat-leaf parsley
1   tablespoon fresh lemon juice

ACCOMPANIMENT:
green salad

Bring water to a boil with salt in a 3-quart saucepan with
a tight-fitting lid. Add salmon fillet and poach at a bare
simmer, covered, until just cooked through, about 4 minutes. Transfer salmon to a plate with a slotted spoon,
reserving poaching liquid, and cover salmon. Return
poaching liquid to a boil and stir in rice. Cook rice, covered, over low heat 15 minutes, or until water is absorbed
and rice is tender.

While rice is cooking, cook onion in butter in a large
skillet over moderately low heat, stirring occasionally,
until softened. Stir in cooked rice and season with salt
and pepper. Break salmon into large pieces and add to
rice mixture with eggs, parsley, and lemon juice. Cook
kedgeree over moderate heat, stirring gently, just until
heated through, about 1 minute.

 Amity Vineyards Willamette Valley, Oregon,
Pinot Blanc 1998

SAFFRON CHICKEN AND CHICKPEA STEW

Serves 4

- 1 medium onion, chopped
- 3 large garlic cloves, minced
- 1 (3-inch) cinnamon stick
- 1/4 teaspoon crumbled saffron threads
- 1/4 teaspoon dried hot red pepper flakes
- 1 bay leaf
- 1 pinch of ground cloves
- 2 teaspoons extra-virgin olive oil
- 1/2 large fennel bulb (sometimes called anise; 6 oz)
- 1 red bell pepper, cut into 1 1/2-inch pieces
- 1 yellow bell pepper, cut into 1 1/2-inch pieces

- 1 3/4 cups canned crushed tomatoes (15-oz can)
- 1/2 cup chicken broth
- 1/2 cup water
- 1 lb skinless boneless chicken breast halves
- 1 1/2 cups canned chickpeas (19-oz can), rinsed, drained, and skins removed
- 3 tablespoons chopped fresh flat-leaf parsley

ACCOMPANIMENT:
fennel pita toasts (page 173)
or bread

Cook onion, garlic, cinnamon stick, saffron, pepper flakes, bay leaf, and clove in oil in a 4-quart heavy saucepan over low heat, stirring occasionally, until onion is softened, about 12 minutes.

Trim fennel stalks flush with bulb, discarding stalks, and trim any discolored outer layers. Cut bulb lengthwise into 1/4-inch wedges. Add fennel and bell peppers to onion mixture and cook, stirring occasionally, 5 minutes. Add tomatoes, broth, and water and simmer, covered, until peppers are tender, about 10 minutes.

Pat chicken dry and cut crosswise into 3/4-inch-thick slices. Season with salt and pepper. Add chicken and chickpeas to vegetable mixture and simmer, stirring occasionally, until chicken is cooked through, about 6 minutes. Stir in parsley and salt and pepper to taste.

Each serving (not including toasts) about 312 calories and 5 grams fat

 Côtes du Rhône Les Abeilles, Jean-Luc Colombo 1998

SHRIMP AND CORN WITH BASIL

Serves 2

2   tablespoons unsalted butter
2   ears corn, kernels cut off ears
½   lb shelled large shrimp
4   scallions, chopped
¼   cup fresh basil, thinly sliced

ACCOMPANIMENTS:
loaf of crusty bread and salad

Melt butter in a large nonstick skillet over moderately
high heat until foam subsides, then sauté corn and
shrimp, stirring, until shrimp are cooked through, 3 to
5 minutes. Stir in scallions and basil and season with salt
and pepper. Recipe may be doubled to serve 4.

Ladoucette Pouilly-Fumé 1998

CHICKEN ROASTED WITH TOMATOES, POTATOES, AND OLIVES

Serves 2

- 7 garlic cloves
- ¼ teaspoon salt
- 2 teaspoons fresh lemon juice
- 3 tablespoons olive oil
- 1 large lemon, thinly sliced crosswise
- 1 chicken breast with skin and bone (1 lb), halved
- 1 lb small (2-inch) red potatoes, quartered
- 4 plum tomatoes, halved lengthwise
- 10 Kalamata or other brine-cured black olives, pitted and thinly sliced lengthwise
- 1 tablespoon fresh rosemary

Preheat oven to 450°F and lightly oil a 13- by 9-inch shallow baking pan.

Mince and mash 2 garlic cloves to a paste with salt. Whisk together garlic paste, lemon juice, and 2 tablespoons oil with salt and pepper to taste in small bowl. Make 2 beds of overlapping lemon slices in pan and put a chicken breast half, skin side up, on each bed. Brush chicken generously with some garlic-lemon mixture and season with salt and pepper.

Toss potatoes, tomatoes, remaining 5 garlic cloves, and remaining tablespoon olive oil in a bowl until coated well. Arrange vegetables around chicken and sprinkle with olives and rosemary.

Roast in middle of oven 15 minutes and brush with remaining garlic-lemon mixture. Roast 10 to 15 minutes more, or until a meat thermometer inserted into chicken registers 175°F.

Discard lemon slices and serve chicken with vegetables, spooning any pan juices over them.

 Pèppoli Chianti Classico, Antinori 1997

SALADS FOR

dinner

The next time you think, "I'd like a salad for dinner tonight," look no further. Here you'll find a variety of no-cook green salads (lettuce or herbs) with plenty of options (namely tuna, vegetables, or smoked chicken); a green salad topped with poached eggs and another with grilled steak; stir-frys (with veggies and tuna, turkey, or pork); and a fabulous pasta salad (featured on our front jacket). Of course, the no-cook salads are ideal in hot weather, but there are no rules here. Let whimsy be your guide.

A NEW CHEF'S SALAD

Serves 4 to 6

1 teaspoon salt
1 red onion, halved lengthwise
   and thinly sliced crosswise
   FOR DRESSING
⅔ cup fresh basil
¼ cup fresh flat-leaf parsley
3 tablespoons mixed fresh herbs
   such as thyme, rosemary, and
   marjoram
1 garlic clove, chopped
3 tablespoons white-wine vinegar
½ teaspoon salt
½ cup olive oil

1 (⅓-lb) piece Parmigiano-
   Reggiano

1 head romaine, torn into
   bite-size pieces
1 small head radicchio, torn into
   bite-size pieces
1 small head frisée, torn into
   bite-size pieces
1 (3-oz) container sunflower
   sprouts
1 (15- to 19-oz) can chickpeas,
   rinsed and drained
1 (1-lb) piece ham, cut into
   thin strips
¾ lb cherry tomatoes, halved
8 radishes, thinly sliced
6 carrots, shredded

Dissolve salt in a medium bowl of ice water and stir in onion. Let onion stand at least 15 minutes and up to 1 hour.

MAKE DRESSING:

While onion is soaking, finely chop herbs and garlic with vinegar and salt in a blender or food processor and, with motor running, add oil in a stream until blended.

Drain onion and pat dry. Shave thin slices from Parmigiano-Reggiano. Toss lettuces, onion, cheese, sprouts, and remaining ingredients in a large bowl. Toss with dressing and salt and pepper to taste.

 Château Routas, Rouvière, Coteaux Varois Rosé 1998

CRISPY ASIAN CHICKEN AND WATERCRESS SALAD

Serves 2

¼ cup hoisin sauce

¼ cup water

1½ tablespoons soy sauce

½ teaspoon finely grated peeled fresh ginger

4 radishes, halved lengthwise and cut crosswise into ⅛-inch-thick slices

2 scallions, cut diagonally into ¼-inch-thick slices

¾ bunch watercress, coarse stems discarded

¾ cup fresh bean sprouts

1 lb boneless chicken thighs with skin

2 tablespoons all-purpose flour

2 tablespoons cornstarch

1 cup vegetable oil for frying

Whisk together hoisin sauce, water, soy sauce, and ginger in a small bowl.

Chill radishes, scallions, watercress, and bean sprouts in a separate bowl.

While vegetables are chilling, pat chicken dry and season with salt. Cut into ¼-inch-thick strips, without removing skin. Stir together flour and cornstarch and add chicken, tossing until coated well. Heat oil in a 12-inch skillet over moderately high heat until hot but not smoking, then fry chicken in batches, separating pieces and turning them occasionally, until crisp and cooked through, 6 to 8 minutes. Transfer with a slotted spoon to paper towels to drain.

Toss chicken with three fourths ginger dressing. Toss vegetables with remaining dressing and combine with chicken.

 Mâcon-Villages Blanc, Tête de Cuvée, Verget 1998

FRISÉE SALAD WITH LARDONS AND POACHED EGGS

Serves 4

The secret to this take on salad lyonnaise is very fresh eggs. (Please note: Serving this salad with runny—not fully cooked—yolks may be of concern if there is a problem with salmonella in your area.) Also, if the slab bacon you're using is lean, add 1 tablespoon vegetable oil to the skillet when cooking.

½   lb frisée, torn into bite-size pieces
6   oz slab bacon or thick-cut bacon slices
2   tablespoons distilled white vinegar
4   large eggs
2   tablespoons chopped shallot
3   tablespoons red-wine vinegar

Put frisée in a large bowl. If using slab bacon, cut lengthwise into ¼-inch-thick slices. Cut bacon crosswise into ¼-inch-thick sticks (*lardons*).

Cook bacon in a heavy skillet over moderate heat, stirring occasionally, until golden and remove from heat.

Have ready another skillet filled with 1 inch warm water. Half-fill a 4-quart saucepan with water and stir in white vinegar. Bring to a bare simmer. Break each egg into a teacup. Slide 1 egg into simmering liquid and immediately push white around yolk with a slotted spoon, moving egg gently. (Egg will become oval, with yolk covered by white.) Add remaining 3 eggs in same manner. Simmer eggs 1½ minutes for runny yolks to 3 minutes for firm yolks. Immediately transfer eggs to skillet of warm water.

Reheat bacon in skillet over moderate heat. Add shallot and cook, stirring, 1 minute. Add red-wine vinegar and boil 5 seconds. Immediately pour hot dressing over frisée and toss with salt and pepper to taste.

Top salad with drained poached eggs and season with salt and pepper. Serve immediately.

 Château Thivin, Côte de Brouilly 1999

GREEK SALAD WITH TUNA

Serves 2

½ English cucumber, halved lengthwise
   and cut crosswise into ¼-inch-thick pieces
½ lb cherry tomatoes, quartered
⅓ cup Kalamata olives, pitted and quartered
3 oz feta, cut into ¼-inch dice
1 (6-oz) can tuna in olive oil (not drained)

Toss together cucumber, tomatoes, olives, feta, tuna with
oil from can, and salt and pepper to taste in a bowl, keeping tuna in large chunks. Recipe may be doubled to
serve 4.

 Santorini Boutari 1999

SMOKED CHICKEN AND SUGAR SNAP PEA SALAD WITH MINT

Serves 4

2	(6-oz) smoked chicken breast halves, skin discarded and chicken cut crosswise into ¼-inch-thick slices
½	lb sugar snap peas, trimmed and cut diagonally into thin slices
1	English cucumber, halved lengthwise, seeded, and cut diagonally into thin slices
3	scallions, cut diagonally into thin slices
¼	cup fresh mint, chopped
1	teaspoon minced peeled fresh ginger
1½	tablespoons olive oil
1½	tablespoons fresh lime juice

Toss together all ingredients and season with salt and pepper.

 Château Souverain Sonoma County Chardonnay 1998

GRILLED STEAK SALAD WITH PICKLE-PEPPER VINAIGRETTE

Serves 2 generously

FOR PICKLE-PEPPER VINAIGRETTE
- 3 tablespoons white-wine vinegar
- 2 tablespoons Dijon mustard
- 3 tablespoons olive oil
- 1 teaspoon sugar
- ¼ cup finely diced red bell pepper
- ¼ cup finely diced peeled and seeded cucumber
- 2 tablespoons finely diced dill pickle
- 2 tablespoons chopped shallot
- 2 tablespoons drained capers

- 1 lb (1¼-inch-thick) boneless beef top loin (strip) steak
- 1 bunch watercress, tough stems discarded

Prepare grill.

MAKE VINAIGRETTE:

Whisk together vinegar, mustard, oil, sugar, and salt to taste. Stir in remaining vinaigrette ingredients and season with pepper.

Season steak with salt and pepper and grill on an oiled rack set 5 to 6 inches over glowing coals about 3 minutes on each side for medium-rare. (Alternatively, grill in a hot well-seasoned ridged grill pan over moderately high heat.) Transfer to a cutting board and let stand 5 minutes. Cut steak into about 12 thin slices with a sharp knife held at a 45° angle.

Spoon vinaigrette generously onto 2 large plates and mound watercress in center. Arrange steak slices on watercress.

 Château de Chamirey, Mercury Rouge 1998

SHRIMP COCKTAIL EXOTIQUE
Serves 4

2   navel oranges
1½ lb medium shrimp (32 total),
    shelled and deveined
2   teaspoons extra-virgin olive oil
¼   teaspoon minced and mashed
    garlic
FOR SAUCE
½   cup mayonnaise
3   tablespoons ketchup
1½ tablespoons Cognac

2   teaspoons fresh lime juice,
    or to taste
½   teaspoon sugar
1   pinch of cayenne

3   firm-ripe California avocados,
    quartered lengthwise, pitted,
    peeled, and cut into ½-inch dice
6   canned hearts of palm, drained,
    rinsed, patted dry, and cut
    crosswise into ½-inch pieces

Cut a slice from top and bottom of each orange with a sharp knife, exposing flesh, and arrange with a cut side down on a cutting board. Cutting from top to bottom, remove peel and pith. Working over a bowl, cut orange sections free from membranes, letting sections drop into bowl, and squeeze in excess juice from membranes.

Plunge shrimp into a large saucepan of boiling salted water and poach at a bare simmer just until firm, 1 to 2 minutes. Drain and transfer to a large bowl. While shrimp are still warm add oil, garlic, and 1 tablespoon juice from orange sections, stirring to coat shrimp. Let cool to room temperature.

MAKE SAUCE:

Whisk together mayonnaise, ketchup, Cognac, lime juice, sugar, and cayenne until smooth.

Transfer orange sections to shrimp mixture with a slotted spoon and add avocado and hearts of palm, folding ingredients together gently.

Divide salad among 4 plates, mounding it, and spoon sauce over salad.

 Joseph Phelps Napa Valley Viognier 1998

THAI GROUND-PORK SALAD WITH MINT AND CILANTRO

Serves 4

This authentic Thai recipe is quite spicy. Adjust the amount of cayenne and Asian fish sauce to taste.

1	bunch fresh cilantro
1	bunch fresh mint
½	small head white or green cabbage (1 lb), cut lengthwise into 4 wedges and core removed
10	oz lean ground pork
3	to 4 tablespoons fresh lime juice
2	small shallots, thinly sliced lengthwise
2	tablespoons plain dry bread crumbs
1	to 2 tablespoons Asian fish sauce (preferably *naam pla*)
⅛	teaspoon cayenne

Chop enough cilantro and mint leaves to measure 2 tablespoons each. Discard tough stems from remaining cilantro and mint and arrange sprigs on a platter. Arrange cabbage wedges on platter.

Stir together pork and 2 tablespoons lime juice in a small saucepan with a fork and cover with cold salted water. Bring to a simmer, stirring with fork to break up meat, and gently simmer until pork is just cooked through, 1 to 2 minutes. Drain well and toss with shallots, chopped herbs, bread crumbs, fish sauce, cayenne, and remaining lime juice to taste.

Transfer salad to a serving bowl and put on platter. Have everyone serve themselves: Arrange sprigs of cilantro and mint on pieces of cabbage and spoon some pork salad on top. Close cabbage around mixture to eat.

Each serving about 215 calories and 12 grams fat

 Baron Knyphausen Rheingau Riesling 1998

CHINESE TURKEY IN JADE

Serves 4

Here we've adapted the classic Chinese dish "squab in jade," in which the meat is minced, stir-fried, and served in "cups" of lettuce.

1   lb lean ground turkey
2   teaspoons honey
4   tablespoons soy sauce
3   tablespoons seasoned rice vinegar
2   tablespoons minced garlic
3   tablespoons finely grated peeled fresh ginger
1   tablespoon Worcestershire sauce
½   cup water
1½ tablespoons sugar
2   teaspoons cornstarch
2   teaspoons vegetable oil

1   (8-oz) can water chestnuts, rinsed, drained, and coarsely chopped
½   cup snow peas, cut diagonally into ½-inch-wide pieces
4   scallions, chopped
½   teaspoon Asian sesame oil
3   heads Bibb lettuce, leaves separated

ACCOMPANIMENTS:

1 cup fresh mint sprigs
1 cup fresh cilantro sprigs
2 cups cooked white rice

Mix together turkey, 1 teaspoon honey, 1 tablespoon each soy sauce, vinegar, and garlic, and 2 tablespoons ginger in a bowl. Marinate 15 minutes.

Whisk together Worcestershire sauce, water, sugar, cornstarch, and remaining teaspoon honey, 3 tablespoons soy sauce, and 2 tablespoons vinegar.

Heat vegetable oil in a wok over moderately high heat until hot but not smoking, then sauté turkey mixture, stirring and breaking up lumps, until just cooked through, about 3 minutes. Transfer with a slotted spoon to cleaned bowl. Stir-fry remaining tablespoon each garlic and ginger in wok 15 seconds. Add water chestnuts and stir-fry 15 seconds. Add turkey mixture, soy-sauce mixture, snow peas, and scallions and stir-fry until sauce is thickened, about 3 minutes. Remove from heat and stir in sesame oil and salt and pepper to taste.

Serve turkey, mint, and cilantro on lettuce leaves accompanied by rice.

Each serving (including rice) about 425 calories and 12 grams fat

St. Supéry Napa Valley Sauvignon Blanc 1999

STIR-FRIED TUNA "CHOP CHOP" SALAD

Serves 4

½	yellow squash	½	cup fresh bean sprouts, stringy root ends trimmed
¾	lb fresh tuna steaks		
2	teaspoons olive oil	1½	tablespoons soy sauce
1	lb asparagus, cut diagonally into ¼-inch pieces	1	teaspoon Chinese chili paste*
1	carrot, cut into ¼-inch dice	1	teaspoon honey
1	small red onion, cut into ¼-inch dice	¼	cup fresh basil, chopped
		¼	cup fresh cilantro, chopped
¼	lb Chinese long beans or green beans, cut into ¼-inch pieces		
2	garlic cloves, minced		
1	tablespoon grated peeled fresh ginger		

ACCOMPANIMENT:
½ cup cooked white or brown rice per serving

*available at Asian markets and many specialty foods shops and supermarkets

Remove peel from squash in ¼-inch-thick strips and cut enough peel into ¼-inch dice to measure ½ cup. Pat tuna dry and cut into ¼-inch dice. Season with salt and pepper.

Heat oil in a large heavy skillet over moderately high heat until hot but not smoking, then stir-fry squash peel, asparagus, carrot, onion, and beans 1 minute. Add tuna, garlic, and ginger and stir-fry until tuna is just cooked through, about 1 minute. Add bean sprouts, soy sauce, chili paste, and honey and stir-fry 15 seconds. Remove from heat and stir in basil and cilantro.

Each serving (including rice) about 284 calories and 7 grams fat

 Iron Horse Green Valley-Sonoma County Pinot Noir 1998

WARM PASTA SALAD WITH BABY SPINACH AND TUNA

Serves 4

1   (6-oz) can light tuna in olive oil,
    drained and crumbled
1   (19-oz) can *cannellini* beans, rinsed
½   English cucumber, quartered lengthwise
    and cut into ½-inch pieces
1   cup halved cherry tomatoes
½   lb *campanelle* or any short curly pasta

For dressing
1   garlic clove
½   teaspoon salt
½   teaspoon chopped fresh rosemary
2   tablespoons fresh lemon juice
¼   cup extra-virgin olive oil

6   cups baby spinach (5-oz package),
    coarse stems discarded
¼   cup capers, rinsed

Toss together tuna, beans, cucumber, and tomatoes in a large bowl.

Cook pasta in a large pot of boiling salted water until al dente, about 10 minutes. Drain pasta and add to tuna mixture.

Make dressing:

Mash garlic to a paste with salt and whisk together with rosemary and lemon juice. Add oil in a slow stream, whisking until emulsified.

Add baby spinach and capers to pasta mixture and toss with dressing.

 Bouchaine Carneros Chardonnay 1998

QUICK STOVE-TOP DISHES

As all short-order cooks know, stove-top cooking gets food on the table *fast*, often in 20 minutes or less. Our main-course dishes are no exception, and they'll even teach you a thing or two about handling your pans. You'll learn to master the following techniques: sautéing (frying in a small amount of fat, then using the pan juices in a sauce), searing (quickly browning foods over high heat to form a crust and enhance flavor), pan-roasting (cooking in a small amount of hot oil over moderate heat in a covered pan to keep foods moist), and stir-frying (keeping chopped ingredients in motion in a thin layer of heated oil until uniformly cooked)—just like a pro.

CORNMEAL-CRUSTED CHICKEN WITH TOASTED CORN SALSA

Serves 2

For salsa

- 1 garlic clove
- 1 pinch of salt
- 2 tablespoons fresh lime juice
- 3 tablespoons extra-virgin olive oil
- 2 cups fresh corn kernels (from 4 ears)
- ¼ cup fresh cilantro, finely chopped
- 1 cup diced peeled mango
- 1 cup diced drained bottled pickled beets
- ¼ cup finely chopped scallions

- 1 whole skinless boneless chicken breast (¾ lb), halved
- ¼ cup yellow cornmeal
- ¼ teaspoon paprika
- ¼ teaspoon cayenne
- 2 teaspoons unsalted butter

Make salsa:

Mince together garlic and salt and whisk together with lime juice, 2 tablespoons oil, and salt and pepper to taste in a bowl. Heat remaining table-spoon oil in a nonstick skillet over moderately high heat until hot but not smoking, then sauté corn, stirring, until deep golden, about 4 minutes. Add corn and remaining salsa ingredients to bowl and toss to combine. (Beets may bleed.)

Pat chicken dry and season with salt and pepper. Stir together cornmeal, paprika, and cayenne on a plate and press chicken into mixture, coating both sides. Heat butter in skillet over moderately high heat until foam subsides, then sauté chicken until golden and cooked through, about 5 minutes on each side.

Serve with salsa.

Photo on page 57

PAN-ROASTED SALMON WITH GINGER AND CURRY

Serves 2

If you're in the mood for an Asian-inspired meal, serve this fish with our pickled cucumber and cabbage (recipe on page 141).

- 2 teaspoons minced peeled fresh ginger
- 1 teaspoon curry powder
- 2 (6-oz) pieces center-cut salmon fillet with skin, patted dry
- 1 tablespoon olive oil
- 3 scallions, chopped

Stir together ginger and curry and season with salt and pepper. Pat spice mixture onto flesh sides of salmon. Heat oil in a large nonstick skillet over moderate heat until hot but not smoking, then cook salmon, skin sides down, covered, 5 minutes. Turn salmon over and cook, covered, until just cooked through, about 2 minutes more. Add scallions to salmon and cook 30 seconds. Recipe may be doubled to serve 4.

Photo opposite

SAUTÉED SEA SCALLOPS WITH MUSTARD SAUCE

Serves 2

¾ lb sea scallops, tough muscles removed
1½ tablespoons olive oil
1 large shallot, minced
¼ cup dry white wine
⅓ cup water
2 tablespoons Dijon mustard
2 tablespoons cold unsalted butter, cut into bits
2 scallion greens, cut diagonally into ¼-inch
     pieces (2 tablespoons)

Pat scallops dry and season with salt and pepper.
Heat oil in a 10- to 12-inch nonstick skillet over
moderately high heat until hot but not smoking,
then sauté scallops until golden and just cooked
through, 1 to 2 minutes on each side. Transfer
scallops with tongs to a plate and keep warm,
covered loosely.

Cook shallot in oil remaining in skillet over
moderate heat, stirring, until softened. Add
wine and boil, stirring and scraping up brown
bits, 1 minute. Stir in water and mustard and
simmer until reduced to about ¼ cup. Add
butter and swirl skillet, returning skillet to heat
as necessary, until butter is just incorporated
into sauce. Season with salt and pepper.

Spoon sauce onto a small platter or 2 plates.
Top with scallops and sprinkle with scallion.

Photo opposite, top

PAN-SEARED HALIBUT WITH SALSA VERDE

Serves 2

2 tablespoons fresh lemon juice
½ teaspoon finely grated fresh lemon zest
2 teaspoons drained capers, chopped
¼ teaspoon minced garlic
¼ cup plus 1 tablespoon extra-virgin olive oil
2 tablespoons chopped fresh cilantro
2 tablespoons chopped fresh flat-leaf parsley
2 (½-inch-thick) halibut steaks with skin (1 lb)

GARNISH:
lemon wedges

Whisk together lemon juice, zest, capers,
garlic, and salt and pepper to taste. Add ¼ cup
oil in a slow stream, whisking constantly
until emulsified, and whisk in herbs.

Pat halibut dry and season with salt and pepper.
Heat remaining tablespoon oil in a nonstick
skillet over moderate heat until hot but not
smoking, then cook halibut, turning once,
until golden brown on both sides and just
cooked through, about 7 minutes total.

Serve halibut topped with *salsa verde*.

Photo opposite, bottom

nonstick skillets

For many of us, the nonstick skillet is the one we turn to again and again, for grilled cheese sandwiches and pan-fried fish and all manner of fried eggs. After all, it's light and easy to handle and a cinch to clean. It also offers the advantage of cooking with very little added fat. Truthfully, you'll need to replace your nonstick pan every couple of years (sooner if severely scratched), but with a little tender loving care it will last longer. Here are a few tips:

- First things first. Be sure to wash your new nonstick pan and dry it thoroughly. After it dries, it should be seasoned with a bit of vegetable oil applied with a paper towel or soft clean cloth.

- Avoid heating an empty pan and cooking with your pan over high heat unless you're boiling or reducing liquids. Similarly, never let the pan boil dry. And it's best not to use nonstick cooking sprays as they tend to burn even at very low temperatures, causing a filmy buildup that interferes with the pan's performance. It's equally important that you use only wood and plastic utensils with your nonstick pan. Sharp-edged tools are strongly discouraged.

- Always wash your pan after each use with nonabrasive materials (*never* use steel wool or scouring pads) and let it dry completely before reseasoning. Layer paper towels between pans if you plan to stack them.

— Ellen Morrissey

FILET MIGNON WITH MUSTARD SAUCE

Serves 2

Crisp potato galettes (page 140) and broccoli rabe (page 140) make ideal accompaniments to this dish.

1	(7-oz) filet mignon (2 inches thick)
½	teaspoon olive oil
1½	tablespoons Cognac
¼	cup beef broth
¼	cup water
2	tablespoons coarse-grained mustard
1	teaspoon unsalted butter

Halve filet crosswise and season with salt and pepper. Heat oil in a small heavy skillet over moderate heat until hot but not smoking, then cook filets 2 to 3 minutes on each side for rare. Let stand on a cutting board, tented loosely with foil, 5 minutes.

While filets are standing, deglaze skillet with Cognac over moderate heat, stirring and scraping up brown bits. Add broth and water and boil until reduced to about ¼ cup. Remove from heat and whisk in mustard, butter, any meat juices from cutting board, and salt and pepper to taste.

Thinly slice filets and serve with sauce. Recipe may be doubled to serve 4.

Each serving (including sauce) about 222 calories and 12 grams fat

Photo left, top

SEARED SEA BASS WITH FRESH HERBS AND LEMON

Serves 2

2	sea bass fillets with skin (7 oz each)
1	teaspoon olive oil
1½	tablespoons unsalted butter
⅓	cup dry white wine
1	tablespoon fresh lemon juice
⅓	cup mixed fresh herbs such as parsley, dill, and chives, chopped

Remove any bones from sea bass with tweezers. Pat fillets dry and score just through skin in 4 places. Diagonally halve each fillet and season with salt and pepper. Heat oil and 1 tablespoon butter in a heavy skillet over moderately high heat until foam subsides, then sear fish, skin sides down, about 3 minutes, or until skin is golden. Turn fish over and cook 2 minutes more, or until just cooked through. Transfer to 2 plates.

Remove skillet from heat and add wine to deglaze, stirring and scraping up any brown bits. Stir in lemon juice, herbs, remaining ½ tablespoon butter, and salt and pepper to taste. Spoon sauce over fish.

Photo opposite, bottom

PAN-ROASTED CHICKEN WITH ORANGES, ROSEMARY, AND ALMONDS

Serves 2

Although Michael Lomonaco uses French-cut chicken breast halves with skin (wing bone is attached and all other breast bones are removed by butcher), boneless breast halves with skin can be substituted.

2	French-cut chicken breast halves with skin or boneless chicken breast halves with skin
2	tablespoons extra-virgin olive oil
1	carrot, finely chopped
1	small white onion, finely chopped
½	cup dry white wine
½	cup low-salt chicken broth
1	tablespoon fresh rosemary, chopped
2	large navel or blood oranges, peel and pith removed and flesh cut into ⅛-inch-thick slices
¼	cup blanched whole almonds, toasted

Pat chicken dry and season with salt and pepper. Heat oil in a large heavy skillet over moderate heat until hot but not smoking, then cook chicken over moderately low heat, skin sides down, until deep golden brown, about 10 minutes. Turn chicken over and cook 6 minutes more.

Transfer chicken with tongs to a plate and pour off all but about 1 tablespoon fat from skillet. Sauté carrot and onion in remaining fat over high heat, stirring, 2 minutes and add wine. Boil wine until reduced by about half and add broth. Bring to a boil and return chicken to skillet, skin sides up. Simmer chicken, covered with lid slightly ajar, 10 minutes and add rosemary and orange slices. Simmer, uncovered, 5 minutes and season with salt and pepper.

Divide chicken between 2 plates and spoon sauce on top. Sprinkle chicken with almonds.

Photo left

PORK CHOPS WITH CORIANDER-CUMIN SPICE RUB

Serves 2

For a delicious, quick accompaniment try our creamy parmesan polenta (recipe on page 153).

1   tablespoon cumin seeds, toasted and coarsely ground
1   tablespoon coriander seeds, toasted and coarsely ground
3   garlic cloves, finely chopped
2   tablespoons olive oil
2   (¾-inch-thick) pork chops
2   tablespoons coarsely chopped fresh cilantro

GARNISH:
lime wedges

Combine cumin, coriander, garlic, and 1 table-spoon oil. Pat pork chops dry and season with salt and pepper. Rub spice mixture on both sides of chops.

Heat remaining tablespoon oil in a large heavy skillet over moderate heat until hot but not smoking, then cook chops until just cooked through, 5 to 7 minutes on each side.

Serve pork chops sprinkled with cilantro. Recipe may be doubled to serve 4.

Photo opposite

CHICKEN STIR-FRY WITH SHIITAKES, SNOW PEAS, AND PEA SHOOTS

Serves 2 generously

½   egg white
2   teaspoons cornstarch
½   teaspoon salt
2   small boneless skinless chicken breast halves (¾ lb total), cut crosswise into very thin slices
¼   cup seasoned rice vinegar
2   tablespoons soy sauce
2   teaspoons sugar
4   to 5 tablespoons vegetable oil
2   teaspoons finely chopped peeled fresh ginger
1   large garlic clove, finely chopped
6   oz shiitake mushrooms, stems discarded and caps cut into ⅓-inch strips
6   oz snow peas, trimmed
1   (4-oz) box pea shoots, tough or leafless stems discarded and remainder cut into 2-inch lengths

Stir together egg white, cornstarch, and salt and stir in chicken. Stir together vinegar, soy sauce, and sugar in another bowl until sugar is dissolved.

Heat a wok over high heat until a bead of water dropped on cooking surface evaporates immediately. Add 2 tablespoons oil, swirling wok to coat evenly, and heat until hot but not smoking. Stir-fry chicken mixture, separating pieces, until just cooked through, 2 to 3 minutes. Transfer chicken to a bowl and wipe wok clean.

Heat wok and add 2 tablespoons oil in same manner. Stir-fry ginger and garlic 30 seconds. Add mushrooms and stir-fry, adding remaining tablespoon oil if necessary, until they begin to soften, about 2 minutes. Add snow peas and stir-fry until crisp-tender, 1 minute. Return chicken to pan and add vinegar mixture, then stir-fry until chicken is heated through, 30 seconds to 1 minute. Remove wok from heat and add pea shoots, tossing to combine.

PAN-SEARED ANCHO CHILE SKIRT STEAK

Serves 4

- 2 large (or 4 small) dried *ancho* or New Mexican chiles (1 oz total)
- ⅔ cup fresh orange juice
- 2 garlic cloves
- 1 tablespoon olive oil
- 1½ lb skirt steak, cut into 4 pieces
- 2 tablespoons vegetable oil

ACCOMPANIMENT:
avocado slices

Heat a large heavy skillet over moderate heat and toast chiles 5 to 10 seconds on each side, pressing down with tongs. Discard stems and seeds and soak chiles in hot water to cover 5 minutes. Drain and tear into pieces. Purée chiles with orange juice, garlic, olive oil, and salt to taste until smooth, about 2 minutes. Transfer half of sauce to a small serving bowl.

Season steak with salt and coat steak generously with remaining sauce.

Heat 2 large heavy skillets over high heat until hot and add 1 tablespoon vegetable oil to each, swirling to coat bottom of pans. Sear steak 2 to 3 minutes on each side for medium-rare. Serve with additional sauce.

STEAMED CLAMS WITH CILANTRO-PARSLEY SAUCE

Serves 2

- 1 medium onion, chopped
- 2 small garlic cloves, thinly sliced
- 1 tablespoon olive oil
- ½ cup dry white wine or dry vermouth
- 2 dozen small hard-shelled clams, cleaned
- 1 cup fresh cilantro
- ½ cup fresh flat-leaf parsley
- 1 tablespoon unsalted butter
- 1 tablespoon fresh lemon juice, or to taste

GARNISH:
fresh cilantro and/or parsley sprigs

ACCOMPANIMENT:
crusty Italian bread

Cook onion and half of garlic in oil in a large heavy saucepan over moderately low heat, stirring, until softened. Add wine and simmer, uncovered, stirring occasionally, 5 minutes. Add clams and steam, covered, over moderately high heat 5 to 7 minutes, transferring them as they open with tongs to a serving bowl and reserving cooking liquid. (Discard any unopened clams.) Keep clams warm.

Blend together cilantro, parsley, butter, remaining garlic, lemon juice, and reserved cooking liquid in a blender until smooth. Pour sauce over clams and toss to combine. Recipe may be doubled to serve 4.

Photo opposite

SEARED SALMON WITH SESAME-SPINACH BOK CHOY

Serves 2

- 2 tablespoons vegetable oil
- 2 (6-oz) salmon fillets
- ¼ lb fresh shiitake mushrooms, stems discarded and caps cut into ¼-inch-thick slices
- 1 garlic clove, chopped
- ½ lb baby bok choy or regular bok choy, trimmed and cut crosswise into 1-inch pieces
- 2½ oz baby spinach, tough stems discarded
- 2½ teaspoons finely grated peeled fresh ginger
- ½ teaspoon dark Asian sesame oil
- 1 teaspoon soy sauce
- 2 teaspoons sesame seeds, toasted

Heat oil in large skillet over moderately high heat until hot but not smoking and cook salmon, flesh sides down, turning once, until golden and just cooked through, about 3 minutes on each side. Transfer to a plate and keep warm, covered. Sauté shiitake over moderately high heat, stirring, until just tender, about 3 minutes. Add garlic and bok choy and sauté, stirring, until bok choy is just tender, about 3 minutes. Remove pan from heat. Toss mixture with spinach, ginger, sesame oil, soy sauce, and salt and pepper to taste.

Top salmon with shiitake mixture and sprinkle with sesame seeds.

Photo right

JALAPEÑO-SPICED MUSSELS

Serves 2

- ¾ lb plum tomatoes (4 or 5), coarsely chopped
- 1 medium onion, coarsely chopped
- 1 fresh jalapeño chile, coarsely chopped (including half of seeds)
- ⅓ cup coarsely chopped fresh cilantro
- 1 tablespoon kosher salt
- ½ cup beer (not dark)
- 2 lb mussels (preferably cultivated), cleaned and beards removed

Purée all ingredients except mussels in a blender or food processor.

Cook tomato mixture and mussels in a 4- to 5-quart pot over moderately high heat, covered, stirring occasionally, until mussels are opened (discard any unopened mussels after 8 minutes).

Each serving about 478 calories and 11 grams fat

SAUTÉED SOLE WITH GREMOLATA BUTTER

Serves 2

1   lemon
¼   cup finely chopped fresh flat-leaf parsley
2   garlic cloves, minced
2   (6-oz) sole or flounder fillets
½   cup all-purpose flour for dredging
½   stick (4 tablespoons) unsalted butter,
    cut into pieces

Finely grate zest of lemon and stir together
with parsley and garlic in a small bowl. Squeeze
2 tablespoons juice from lemon into another
small bowl and set aside. Season fish with salt
and pepper and dredge in flour.

Heat half of butter in a large nonstick skillet over
moderately high heat until foam subsides and
cook fish 1 to 1½ minutes on each side, or until
golden and just cooked through. Transfer to
a platter.

Add lemon juice, remaining butter, and *gremolata*
to pan and cook over moderate heat, shaking pan,
until butter is melted. Season with salt and pepper
and pour over fish.

SEARED TUNA STEAKS WITH RADISH SPROUTS AND SOY BROTH

Serves 2

FOR SOY BROTH
¾   cup water
2   tablespoons soy sauce
2   teaspoons sugar
1   teaspoon seasoned rice vinegar
¼   teaspoon salt
¼   teaspoon sesame oil
2   (⅛-inch-thick) slices peeled fresh ginger,
    cut into julienne strips
1   scallion, thinly sliced
2   mushrooms, thinly sliced

2   (5-oz) pieces tuna steak (1- to 1¼-inch-thick)
1   teaspoon vegetable oil
2   oz radish sprouts (top 2 inches only)

MAKE BROTH:
Simmer broth ingredients in a small saucepan,
stirring until sugar is dissolved. Keep warm.

Season tuna with salt. Heat a medium nonstick
skillet over moderately high heat until hot and
add oil, swirling pan to coat bottom. Sear tuna
2 minutes on each side for medium-rare and,
holding 1 steak at a time with tongs, sear edges
a few seconds.

Pour broth with scallions and mushrooms into
2 soup plates and stand radish sprouts in broth
off to one side. Diagonally halve tuna steaks and
prop one half on top of other in middle of plates.

Each serving about 296 calories and 10 grams fat

FRIED COD TACOS

Serves 4 to 6

- 1   qt vegetable oil
- 12   to 16 corn tortillas
- 1   cup all-purpose flour
- 2   teaspoons salt
- 1   cup beer (not dark)
- 1   lb cod fillet, cut into 3- by 1-inch strips

ACCOMPANIMENTS:
shredded lettuce
sour cream or *chipotle* yogurt sauce (page 89)
avocado slices
chopped or sliced radish
bottled green salsa*
lime wedges

We recommend Rick Bayless's salsas, available at specialty foods stores and some supermarkets.

Preheat oven to 350°F.

Heat 1 inch oil in a 10-inch wide heavy pot (2 to 3 inches deep) over moderate heat until a deep-fat thermometer registers 360°F.

Separate tortillas and make stacks of 6 to 8. Wrap each stack in aluminum foil and heat in oven 12 to 15 minutes.

While tortillas are warming, stir together flour and salt in a large bowl, then stir in beer (batter will be thick). Gently stir fish into batter to coat. Lift each piece of fish out of batter, wiping any excess off on side of bowl, and fry in batches, turning once or twice, until golden, 4 to 5 minutes. Transfer to paper towels to drain.

Increase oil temperature to 375°F and refry fish in batches, turning once or twice, until golden brown and crisp, about 1 minute more. Drain on paper towels.

Assemble tacos with warm tortillas, fish, and accompaniments.

SPICY PORK STIR-FRY WITH BROCCOLI AND GINGER

Serves 2 generously

- 2   tablespoons soy sauce
- 1   tablespoon medium-dry Sherry
- 2   teaspoons cornstarch
- 1/2   lb pork loin, thinly sliced across the grain and cut into julienne strips
- 1   bunch broccoli
- 4   tablespoons vegetable oil
- 1   large garlic clove, finely chopped
- 1   (2-inch) piece peeled fresh ginger, thinly sliced and cut into julienne strips
- 1/2   teaspoon dried hot red pepper flakes
- 1/2   cup chicken broth
- 1   teaspoon sugar

Stir together 1 tablespoon soy sauce, Sherry, and 1 teaspoon cornstarch and stir in pork.

Cut broccoli into small florets. Peel and cut tender sections of stems (top halves) into thin slices.

Heat a wok or nonstick skillet over high heat until a bead of water dropped on cooking surface evaporates immediately. Add 2 tablespoons oil, swirling wok to coat evenly, and heat until hot but not smoking. Add pork mixture and stir-fry until cooked through, 2 minutes. Transfer to a bowl and wipe wok clean.

Heat wok and add remaining 2 tablespoons oil in same manner. Add garlic, ginger, and red pepper flakes and stir-fry 30 seconds. Add broccoli and stir-fry 2 minutes. Add 1/4 cup chicken broth and cook, covered, 1 minute, or until broccoli is crisp-tender.

Stir together remaining tablespoon soy sauce, remaining 1/4 cup broth, remaining teaspoon cornstarch, and sugar, then add to pan with pork and stir-fry 1 minute.

PAN-BRAISED SHRIMP WITH FETA

Serves 2

¾ lb medium shelled and cleaned shrimp
1 teaspoon kosher salt
2 garlic cloves, finely chopped
¾ teaspoon dried oregano, crumbled
¼ cup extra-virgin olive oil
¼ lb coarsely crumbled feta

ACCOMPANIMENT:
warm crusty bread

Toss shrimp with kosher salt and pepper to taste. Cook garlic and oregano in oil in a large nonstick skillet over moderately low heat, stirring, until fragrant. Add shrimp, stirring to coat, and cook, covered, turning shrimp once, until just cooked through, 5 to 7 minutes. Sprinkle feta over shrimp and season with pepper.

SEARED SESAME SCALLOPS WITH PEA AND MINT COUSCOUS

Serves 2

FOR COUSCOUS
⅔ cup water
½ teaspoon salt
½ cup frozen peas
⅔ cup couscous

3 tablespoons sesame seeds
1½ teaspoons kosher salt
⅛ teaspoon freshly ground black pepper
12 large sea scallops (10 oz), tough muscles removed
1½ tablespoons vegetable oil
1 tablespoon chopped fresh mint
2 teaspoons fresh lemon juice

GARNISH:
lemon wedges

MAKE COUSCOUS:
Bring water with salt to a boil in a small saucepan. Add peas and return water to a boil. Stir in couscous. Cover pan and immediately remove from heat. Let couscous stand, covered, 5 minutes.

While couscous is standing, stir together sesame seeds, salt, and pepper. Pat scallops dry. Dip flat sides of each scallop in sesame mixture. Heat oil in a 12-inch nonstick skillet over moderately high heat until hot but not smoking, then sauté scallops on flat sides until sesame seeds are golden and scallops are just cooked through, about 4 minutes total.

Fluff couscous with a fork and stir in mint, lemon juice, and salt and pepper to taste.

Serve couscous topped with scallops.

Photo left

to season cast iron

If you didn't inherit a well-seasoned cast-iron skillet or snag one at a yard sale, you've just found next winter's project. You will need to spend chunks of time oiling and baking your skillet until it loses its gray color and acquires a lacquer-hard black crust.

The first step is to wash the skillet well, using soap and a scouring pad to scrub off its protective coating. (This is the only time soap should ever touch the skillet.) Dry the pan thoroughly, either over a pilot light or upside down in a warm oven. Now it's time to move on to oiling. Some cooks swear by safflower; others, Crisco or peanut. Whatever. Put a *small amount* on a paper towel and rub it around inside the skillet, working it into every pore and pit. (Many people oil the outside of the skillet, including the handle, as well.) Bake the skillet in a preheated 275° F oven for five hours. A couple of five-hour sessions will result in a slightly tacky, caramel-colored hard finish. You'll eventually achieve a black patina that will prevent any oxygen from reaching the iron and causing rust.

As for the cleanup, "never soak, never scour" is our mantra. And it pays to keep control of your pan—you wouldn't want that hard-won black patina scrubbed off by a well-meaning (and energetic or crazy-in-love) guest. To clean, hold the skillet under hot water and "sand" it with an abrasive nylon pad (and a handful of coarse salt, if the pan's encrusted). No soap, no steel wool, no dishwasher. Dry your pan *completely* (see above) and—for the first year—after it has cooled, lightly rub it down with oil before storing it in a dry place. If you want to keep a set nested together, separate the skillets with paper towels to absorb any stray beads of moisture and to prevent scratches. They're family heirlooms, you know.

—Jane Daniels Lear

CORN, SCALLION, AND POTATO FRITTATA

Serves 4 (light main course)

1   bunch scallions, white and green parts
    sliced separately
2   garlic cloves, minced
3   tablespoons olive oil
1   large russet (baking) potato, peeled
    and cut into 1/4-inch dice
2   cups corn kernels (10 oz), thawed if frozen
4   large eggs
4   oz mozzarella, coarsely grated

Cook white part of scallions and garlic in 2
tablespoons oil in a 10-inch nonstick skillet over
moderate heat, stirring, until softened, about
2 minutes. Add potato and cook over moderately
low heat, stirring, until tender, 10 minutes. Add
corn and salt and pepper to taste and cook, stirring, 1 minute for thawed corn or 2 minutes
for fresh.

Whisk together eggs, mozzarella, and salt
and pepper to taste. Stir in potato mixture
and scallion greens.

Heat remaining tablespoon oil in clean skillet
over moderately high heat until hot but not
smoking. Cook egg mixture over moderate heat,
without stirring, shaking skillet once or twice
to loosen frittata, until underside is golden
but top is still wet, about 6 minutes.

Preheat broiler.

Broil frittata 3 inches from heat (if skillet is
not ovenproof, cover handle with a double layer
of foil) until top is just set and golden, about
2 minutes. Slide onto a plate and cool to warm
or room temperature.

Cut into wedges to serve.

VEAL SCALLOPINI WITH MUSHROOMS AND MARSALA

Serves 4

1 1/2   lb veal medallions
    1   cup all-purpose flour
1 1/2   tablespoons vegetable oil
2 1/2   tablespoons unsalted butter
  1/2   lb mushrooms, trimmed and thinly sliced
  1/2   cup dry Marsala
  1/4   cup heavy cream

GARNISH:
lemon wedges

Preheat oven to 200°F.

Pat veal dry. Season half of veal with salt and
pepper and dredge in flour, shaking off excess.
Heat oil and 1 1/2 tablespoons butter in a 12-inch
nonstick skillet over moderately high heat until
foam subsides and sauté veal until golden and
just cooked through, about 1 minute on each side.
Transfer to an ovenproof dish and keep warm
in oven. Season and dredge remaining veal and
sauté in fat in pan in same manner. Transfer
to dish in oven.

Add remaining tablespoon butter to pan and heat
over moderately high heat until foam subsides.
Sauté mushrooms, stirring, until softened, about
2 minutes. Add Marsala and simmer, stirring and
scraping up any brown bits, until reduced by half,
about 2 minutes. Add cream and salt and pepper
to taste and cook until thickened slightly, about
2 minutes.

Pour sauce over veal and serve.

SMOKED SALMON FRITTATA WITH GOAT CHEESE

Serves 2

3   asparagus stalks, trimmed
1   medium Yukon Gold or other boiling potato, peeled and cut into ¼-inch-thick slices
1   cup spinach, coarse stems discarded
3   large eggs
1   plum tomato, peeled, seeded, and cut into ¼-inch dice
2   small mushrooms, thinly sliced
1   scallion, thinly sliced
   Freshly ground white pepper to taste
1   tablespoon olive oil
3   oz sliced smoked salmon, cut into 1-inch squares
1   oz soft mild goat cheese

Cook asparagus in a saucepan of boiling salted water 3 minutes and transfer to an ice water bath with a slotted spoon to stop cooking. Cut asparagus into 1-inch pieces. Cook potato in boiling water 3 minutes and transfer to a sieve to drain. Pat potato dry. Cook spinach in boiling water 1 minute and drain in sieve. Press as much water as possible out of spinach and finely chop.

Preheat broiler.

Whisk eggs in a large bowl and stir in asparagus, tomato, spinach, mushrooms, scallion, and white pepper and salt to taste.

Heat oil in a 9- to 10-inch ovenproof nonstick skillet over moderately high heat, then sauté potatoes in one layer until golden, about 3 minutes on each side. Pour egg mixture over potatoes and transfer skillet to broiler. Broil 5 to 6 inches from heat until top is browned and egg is set, 3 to 4 minutes.

Slide frittata onto a plate and top with salmon. Crumble goat cheese over frittata.

Photo right

LEMON-GARLIC LAMB CHOPS WITH YOGURT SAUCE

Serves 4

FOR YOGURT SAUCE
1   cup plain yogurt
1   garlic clove, minced
2   tablespoons chopped fresh mint
FOR CHOPS
¼   cup fresh lemon juice
2   large garlic cloves, chopped
½   teaspoon dried oregano
3   tablespoons olive oil
4   (½-inch-thick) shoulder lamb chops
1   tablespoon water

MAKE SAUCE:
Drain yogurt in a sieve lined with a double layer of cheesecloth 20 minutes. Stir together with garlic, mint, and salt and pepper to taste.

PREPARE CHOPS:
While yogurt drains, stir together lemon juice, garlic, oregano, and 2 tablespoons oil in a shallow baking dish. Add lamb chops, turning to coat, and marinate 20 minutes.

Remove lamb from marinade, reserving marinade, and season with salt and pepper. Heat remaining tablespoon oil in a 12-inch nonstick skillet over moderately high heat until hot but not smoking, then sauté chops in 2 batches, without crowding, about 2 minutes on each side for medium-rare. Transfer to plates. Boil reserved marinade in skillet with water 1 minute and pour over chops. Serve chops with yogurt sauce.

VEGETABLE COUSCOUS

Serves 4

FOR VEGETABLES

2 tablespoons extra-virgin olive oil
3/4 lb onions (2 medium), peeled and cut into 1-inch pieces
3/4 lb turnips (2 medium), peeled and cut into 1-inch pieces
1 bunch carrots (3/4 lb), peeled and cut diagonally into 1-inch pieces
1 red bell pepper, cut into 1-inch pieces
1 teaspoon ground cumin
1/2 teaspoon caraway seeds, ground
1 teaspoon salt
1/2 teaspoon dried hot red pepper flakes
2 large garlic cloves, finely chopped
3/4 lb zucchini (2 medium), cut into 1-inch pieces
1 cup water
1 cup V-8 juice
2 tablespoons chopped fresh mint

FOR COUSCOUS

2 cups water
1 teaspoon salt
1/8 teaspoon ground turmeric
1/8 teaspoon cinnamon
1 (10-oz) box couscous

COOK VEGETABLES:

Heat oil in a 4-quart heavy pot over moderate heat until hot but not smoking and add onions, turnips, carrots, bell pepper, cumin, caraway, salt, and red pepper flakes, stirring to coat vegetables with oil and spices. Cover pan and cook over moderate heat, stirring occasionally, 15 minutes.

Add garlic and zucchini and cook, stirring, 1 minute. Stir in 1 cup water and V-8 juice and simmer over moderate heat, covered, stirring occasionally, until vegetables are tender, 10 to 15 minutes. Season with salt and pepper and sprinkle with mint.

PREPARE COUSCOUS:

While vegetables are simmering, bring 2 cups water to a boil with salt, turmeric, and cinnamon. Put couscous in a large bowl and pour boiling-water mixture over couscous, stirring to combine. Let stand, uncovered, 5 minutes and fluff with a fork. Let couscous stand, uncovered, 5 minutes more and fluff with a fork again.

Serve couscous with vegetables.

Each serving about 467 calories and 9 grams fat

SWEET ITALIAN SAUSAGE WITH FENNEL AND ONION

Serves 4

8 sweet Italian sausages (1 1/3 lb total)
1 large onion, cut lengthwise into 1/4-inch-thick slices
1 medium to large fennel bulb (sometimes called anise), fronds chopped, stalks removed, and bulb halved, cored, and cut into 1/4-inch-thick slices
1 teaspoon salt
2 tablespoons extra-virgin olive oil

Prick sausages and cook in a heavy skillet over moderately low heat until browned on all sides and cooked through, about 20 minutes.

While sausages are simmering, cook onion, fennel bulb, and salt in oil in a large nonstick skillet over moderately high heat, stirring, until softened, about 8 minutes. Cover skillet and cook, stirring occasionally, until tender, about 8 minutes more. Stir in fennel fronds and serve mixture with sausages.

QUICK GrILLS

There's nothing quite like the seared, locked-in flavor that comes from cooking on the grill. Whether you're grilling outside (with charcoal or gas) or indoors (with a stove-top grill pan), you can be assured of a meal that is flavorful and fast—with little clean-up required. From grilled salmon steaks with ginger butter to grilled turkey cutlets, you'll have plenty of fabulous options. And, for those carefree times when you just want to throw something on the grill, take a look at our handy chart, complete with ideal thicknesses for various cuts of foods and grilling times for each. Luscious toppings also are here for the choosing.

GRILLED STRIP STEAKS WITH OLIVE-OREGANO RELISH

Serves 2

⅓ cup drained Kalamata or other brine-cured black olives, pitted and coarsely chopped
2 tablespoons finely chopped red onion
2 teaspoons minced fresh oregano
2 teaspoons extra-virgin olive oil
2 (¾-inch-thick) boneless beef loin (strip) or rib-eye steaks (½ lb each)

Prepare grill.

Stir together olives, onion, oregano, oil, and salt and pepper to taste. Pat steaks dry and season with salt and pepper. Grill steaks on an oiled rack set 5 to 6 inches over glowing coals about 4 minutes on each side for medium-rare. (Alternatively, grill steaks in a hot oiled well-seasoned ridged grill pan over moderately high heat.)

Serve steaks topped with relish.

Photo on page 77

GRILLED LAMB AND CHERRY TOMATO KEBABS WITH GUACAMOLE

Serves 4

For guacamole
2 ripe California avocados
1 yellow bell pepper, finely chopped
½ cup finely chopped red onion
¼ cup finely chopped fresh cilantro
1 teaspoon minced fresh green chile, such as *serrano* or jalapeño
3 tablespoons fresh lemon juice
1½ teaspoons kosher salt
For kebabs
2 lb boneless lamb shoulder or leg of lamb, cut into 32 (1¼-inch) pieces
24 red or yellow cherry tomatoes
8 (10-inch) bamboo skewers, soaked in water to cover 15 minutes

Vegetable oil for brushing

Prepare grill.

Make guacamole:
Halve, pit, and finely chop avocados and toss with remaining guacamole ingredients.

Make kebabs:
Thread 4 lamb pieces and 3 tomatoes alternately onto skewers. Brush with oil and season with salt and pepper. Grill on an oiled rack set 5 to 6 inches over glowing coals 6 minutes on each side for medium-rare.

Serve kebabs over guacamole.

CHARCOAL GRILLING TIPS

Below are a few helpful tips that will ensure success at the grill. You'll soon realize that grilling over fire is not an exact science—it is a skill developed over time. With experience, you'll be able to judge the heat of the coals and know how to handle flare-ups. Then, too, weather and the amount of food on the rack will affect grilling times. Not to worry, this is all part of the joy of grilling—just remember to keep an eye on the grill!

1. Hardwood lump charcoal is the best fuel for grilling because it imparts flavor without leaving a chemical taste in the food.

2. Build a fire as large as the surface of the food to be grilled. Instead of spreading coals out into an even layer, build a 4-inch deep bed of coals on one side of the kettle, then taper down to a 2-inch deep bed on the other side of the kettle. This will give you varying heats to grill the food and allow transferring to cooler areas if overbrowning occurs.

3. Make sure your rack is clean by putting it over the hot coals a couple of minutes before grilling and using a metal brush to scrape off any food particles. Then brush the rack with a light coating of vegetable oil.

4. A general guideline for judging when the coals are ready is to allow from 30 to 40 minutes from the time of lighting. Judging temperature of the coals is accomplished by holding your hand about 5 inches above the rack: if you can hold it there 5 to 6 seconds, you have a moderately low fire; 3 to 4 seconds, a moderate fire; and 1 to 2 seconds, a very hot fire.

5. Don't crowd food on the grill—putting too much on at one time makes it difficult for food to brown.

—Alexis Touchet

GRILLED INDIAN-SPICED WHOLE RED SNAPPER WITH MANGO RAITA

Serves 4

In order to cook the whole fish properly without over-charring the skin, grill over moderately hot coals (see grilling tip #4 on page 79).

For mango raita
2   tablespoons dessicated coconut*
2   tablespoons water
¼   teaspoon ground cumin
1   tablespoon vegetable oil
½   teaspoon black mustard seeds*
1   fresh hot green chile, minced
8   fresh or frozen curry leaves*
1   (8-oz) container plain yogurt
1   mango, pitted, peeled, and cut into ½-inch pieces

For spice rub
2   tablespoons ground coriander
2   teaspoons kosher salt
1   teaspoon ground cumin
½   teaspoon cayenne
½   teaspoon turmeric
1   tablespoon vegetable oil

1   (3- to 3¼-lb) whole red snapper, cleaned

available at Indian markets and by mail order from Kalustyan's, (212) 685-3451

Prepare grill.

Make raita:
Blend coconut, water, and cumin to a coarse paste in a food processor. Heat oil in a small saucepan over moderate heat until hot but not smoking and add mustard seeds. When seeds begin to pop, add chile, curry leaves, and coconut paste and cook, stirring, over moderately low heat, until liquid is evaporated, about 30 seconds. Stir together yogurt, mango, chile mixture, and salt to taste in a bowl.

Make spice rub:
Stir together all spice rub ingredients.

Make 3 (2-inch) diagonal cuts on each side of fish and pat dry. Rub spice mixture onto fish and into cuts. Grill fish on an oiled rack set 5 to 6 inches over moderately hot coals until browned and just cooked through, turning once with two large metal spatulas, 20 to 25 minutes total. Check cuts in fish for doneness.

Discard curry leaves from *raita* and serve with fish.

GRILLED SALMON STEAKS WITH GINGER BUTTER

Serves 8

1   stick (½ cup) unsalted butter, softened
2   tablespoons finely grated peeled fresh ginger
8   (1-inch-thick) salmon steaks (½ lb each)

Garnishes:
fresh parsley sprigs and lime wedges

Stir together butter, ginger, and salt and pepper to taste. Wrap half of ginger butter in plastic wrap and form into a 6-inch log. Chill log, wrapped, 20 minutes, or until firm enough to slice.

Prepare grill.

Melt remaining ginger butter and brush half on 1 side of salmon steaks. Grill salmon, buttered sides down, on an oiled rack set 5 to 6 inches over glowing coals 4 minutes. Brush salmon with remaining melted ginger butter and turn over. Grill salmon 4 minutes more, or until it just flakes.

Cut ginger-butter log into 8 rounds. Top salmon with butter rounds.

Photo opposite, top

RIB-EYE STEAK
WITH STILTON SAUCE
Serves 2 or 3

¼ lb Stilton (½ cup), softened
½ stick (¼ cup) unsalted butter, softened
¾ cup dry white wine
2 teaspoons freeze-dried green peppercorns
½ cup heavy cream
2 teaspoons minced fresh flat-leaf parsley
1 lb (1-inch-thick) rib-eye steak

Garnish:
watercress sprigs

Cream together cheese and butter until smooth.
Boil wine with peppercorns in a saucepan until
reduced to about 1 tablespoon. Add cream and
boil until reduced by half. Reduce heat to
moderately low and whisk in cheese mixture,
a little at a time. Whisk in parsley. Remove
from heat and keep sauce warm.

Pat steak dry and season with salt and pepper.
Heat a well-seasoned ridged grill pan over
moderately high heat until hot, then cook steak
4 to 5 minutes on each side for medium-rare.
Let stand on a cutting board 10 minutes and
cut into thin slices.

Serve steak with sauce.

Photo left, below

STOVE-TOP GRILL PANS

Stove-top grill pans have become wildly popular among cooks who crave the smoky flavor of grilled foods all year long. After all, most die-hard outdoor grilling enthusiasts eventually have to come indoors. And for those among us who lack a backyard grill (or a backyard, for that matter), these handy pans are heaven-sent.

While grill pans come in a variety of shapes and sizes, their basic design does not vary greatly—all have shallow or minimal sides and raised ridges on the bottom that conduct heat and create the characteristic grill marks. *Gourmet*'s food editors prefer cast-iron grill pans to those with nonstick surfaces and generally avoid using nonstick cooking sprays, opting instead to lightly brush their pans with vegetable oil before adding food.

When following a recipe designed for cooking on an outdoor grill, you'll need to adjust cooking times for the grill pan (see our chart on page 84). As a general rule, foods that are less than 1½ inches thick work best in a stove-top grill pan because they cook quickly and therefore tend not to create a lot of smoke in the kitchen. Also, because the pans are fairly small, cooking in batches is often necessary.

Be sure to clean your grill pan with a plastic bristle brush and hot water (*never* dish detergent) and place it back on the stove over low heat or in the oven to allow it to dry thoroughly. You might then want to go the extra step and give your pan a light brush of vegetable oil.

Although you'd probably never mistake a food cooked on a grill pan for one cooked on an outdoor grill, you'll certainly appreciate the distinctively caramelized flavor the grill pan delivers. In fact, considering the year-round convenience and easy cleanup and storage of this pan, it's likely to become a serious contender for your favorite kitchen tool.

—Ellen Morrissey

GRILLED TURKEY CUTLETS TERIYAKI

Serves 4

Boiling the marinade after the cutlets have been removed is necessary for food safety reasons and it also slightly thickens the marinade so it can be used as a sauce.

FOR MARINADE
- ⅔ cup soy sauce
- ⅓ cup packed light brown sugar
- ¼ cup cider vinegar
- ¼ cup *mirin* (Japanese sweet rice wine) or medium-dry Sherry
- 2 garlic cloves, finely chopped
- 2 tablespoons finely chopped peeled fresh ginger

1½ lb (¼- to ½-inch-thick) turkey cutlets

Prepare grill.

MAKE MARINADE:
Simmer all marinade ingredients in a 2-quart saucepan, stirring until sugar is dissolved, until reduced to about 1¼ cups, about 5 minutes. Cool marinade in a bowl set in a larger bowl of ice and cold water.

Put turkey cutlets and marinade in a sealable plastic bag, pressing out excess air, and marinate 15 minutes. Pour marinade into a saucepan and boil 5 minutes. Grill cutlets on an oiled rack set 5 to 6 inches over glowing coals 1½ minutes on each side, or until just cooked through.

Serve cutlets with teriyaki sauce.

GRILLED PORTABELLA MUSHROOMS WITH HERBED SOUR CREAM

Serves 4

- 4 (4- to 5-inch) portabella mushrooms, stems discarded
- 2 tablespoons olive oil
- ¼ cup pine nuts, toasted
- ⅓ cup sour cream
- 2 tablespoons finely chopped fresh basil
- 2 tablespoons finely chopped fresh flat-leaf parsley
- 2 tablespoons thinly sliced fresh chives
- 1 teaspoon finely chopped fresh thyme

Prepare grill.

Brush both sides of mushrooms lightly with oil and season stem sides with salt and pepper. Grill mushrooms, stem sides up, on an oiled rack set 5 to 6 inches over glowing coals until grill marks appear on surface, 2 to 3 minutes. Turn mushrooms over and grill until tender, 2 to 3 minutes.

While mushrooms are grilling, finely chop half of pine nuts. Stir together sour cream, herbs, and salt and pepper to taste. Spread sour cream over stem sides of mushrooms and sprinkle with whole and chopped pine nuts.

GRILLING (INDOORS AND OUT)

Use the chart below to shop for the ideal thickness or weight of the foods to be grilled, season them as suggested, then grill for the recommended time. All our outdoor grilling was tested on both a charcoal and a gas grill: The gas grill temperature varied from moderate to moderately high heat which was adjusted to avoid overbrowning; the charcoal fire was built to allow transferring the food to cooler areas if flare-ups or overbrowning occurred (see grilling tip #2 on page 79). If you are grilling on a windy or cold day, you'll need to adjust cooking times. When grilling indoors on a grill pan you may need to cook in batches. Grilled food may be kept warm in a 250°F oven, but you should know that the food will continue to cook.

	FOOD TO BE GRILLED	OUTDOOR GRILLING TIME (charcoal or gas grill)	INDOOR GRILLING TIME (grill pan)
PORK CHOPS	4 center-cut rib chops with bone, each 1¼ inches thick, seasoned with salt and pepper	8 to 9 minutes per side, or until a meat thermometer registers 155°F. Let stand off heat, loosely covered, 5 minutes.	Sear 2 minutes per side over high heat, cover and grill over moderate heat until a meat thermometer registers 155°F, 6 to 7 minutes per side. Let stand off heat, loosely covered, 5 minutes.
PORK TENDERLOIN	2 pork tenderloins, 1½ to 2 pounds total, brushed lightly with oil and seasoned with salt and pepper	15 to 20 minutes total, turning to expose all sides every 4 minutes, until a meat thermometer registers 155°F. Let stand off heat, loosely covered, 5 minutes.	Halve, if necessary, to fit pan; sear each side, 2 minutes per side over high heat, then cover and grill over moderate heat until a meat thermometer registers 155°F, 3 to 4 minutes per side. Let stand off heat, loosely covered, 5 minutes.
LAMB CHOPS	8 rib lamb chops, each 1-inch thick, seasoned with salt and pepper	3 minutes per side for medium rare. Let stand off heat, loosely covered, 5 minutes.	Grill 3 minutes per side over moderately high heat, uncovered; then 1 minute more, covered, for medium rare. Let stand off heat, loosely covered, 5 minutes.
FLANK STEAK	1½ pound flank steak (note: this cut is thicker on one end), brushed lightly with oil and seasoned with salt and pepper	6 minutes per side for medium rare on thick end and medium on thin end, then let stand off heat, loosely covered, 5 minutes.	Halve into thick and thinner pieces and grill in 2 batches: Thicker piece 5 minutes per side over moderately high heat, then 2 minutes per side, covered, over moderate heat for medium rare. Grill thinner piece 5 minutes per side over moderately high heat; then 1 minute more, covered, over moderate heat for medium rare.

FOOD TO BE GRILLED	OUTDOOR GRILLING TIME *charcoal or gas grill*	INDOOR GRILLING TIME *grill pan*
CHICKEN BREASTS		
2 whole chicken breasts **with skin and bones** (1¼ pounds per whole breast), each halved and seasoned with salt and pepper	6 minutes per side, skin side down first, or until a meat thermometer registers 160°F. Let stand off heat, loosely covered, 5 minutes.	Grill in batches, two breast halves at a time: 5 minutes skin side down over moderately high heat. Turn and grill over moderate heat, covered, 6 to 8 minutes per side, or until a meat thermometer registers 160°F. Let stand off heat, loosely covered, 5 minutes.
2 whole **boneless skinless** chicken breasts (¾ pound per whole breast), each halved and brushed lightly with oil and seasoned with salt and pepper	4 minutes per side, or until a meat thermometer registers 160°F. Let stand off heat, loosely covered, 5 minutes.	Grill in batches, two breast halves at a time: 2½ minutes per side over moderately high heat, turn and grill over moderate heat, covered, 2 minutes per side, or until a meat thermometer registers 160°F. Let stand off heat, loosely covered, 5 minutes.
CHICKEN THIGHS		
12 chicken thighs **with skin and bones,** seasoned with salt and pepper	6 to 7 minutes per side, skin sides down first, or until just cooked through	Grill in two batches: 4½ minutes per side over moderately high heat, then 2½ minutes per side over moderate heat, covered.
12 **boneless skinless** chicken thighs, brushed lightly with oil and seasoned with salt and pepper	4 minutes per side, or until just cooked through	Grill in two batches: 4 minutes per side, or until just cooked through.
HALIBUT		
4 (1-inch thick) halibut steaks, each ½ pound, brushed lightly with oil and seasoned with salt and pepper	3½ minutes per side, or until just cooked through (flesh should be opaque)	Grill in two batches: 4 minutes per side over moderately high heat, or until just cooked through (flesh should be opaque).
TUNA		
4 (1-inch thick) tuna steaks, each ½ pound, brushed lightly with oil and seasoned with salt and pepper	2 minutes per side for medium	Grill in batches: 2 minutes per side, partially covered, for medium.
SHRIMP		
1½ pounds large shrimp in shell (about 36), brushed lightly with oil and seasoned with salt and pepper	Soak 9 (10-inch) bamboo skewers in water to cover 15 minutes. Thread 4 shrimp onto each skewer, then grill 1½ minutes per side.	Grill in batches: 1½ minutes per side (do not use skewers), over moderately high heat, partially covered. (Transfer to a bowl and keep covered while grilling remaining shrimp.)

WATERMELON, CANTALOUPE, AND RED PEPPER SALSA
Makes about 4 cups

This summery condiment tastes great with any grilled chicken, lean beef, or seafood. Or, simply serve it with a bowl of tortilla chips.

1 (1-lb) piece watermelon, rind and seeds removed and cut into ¼-inch dice
1 (1-lb) piece cantaloupe, rind and seeds removed and cut into ¼-inch dice
½ red bell pepper, cut into ¼-inch dice
½ small sweet onion such as Vidalia, finely chopped
⅓ cup fresh cilantro, finely chopped
½ fresh jalapeño chile, finely chopped with seeds (wear rubber gloves)
2 tablespoons chopped fresh mint
1 tablespoon fresh lime juice

Toss together all ingredients and season with salt.

Each 1-cup serving about 56 calories and less than 1 gram fat

Photo opposite, bottom

TOMATILLO CELERY SALSA
Makes about 3 cups

We loved this refreshing condiment paired with both grilled beef and shrimp.

1 lb fresh tomatillos, husks removed
4 celery ribs, cut into ¼-inch dice
1 cup fresh cilantro, finely chopped
6 radishes, sliced and cut into julienne strips
1 tablespoon fresh lemon juice

Rinse tomatillos under warm water to remove stickiness. Pat dry and cut about three fourths

into ¼-inch dice. Purée remaining tomatillos in a blender or food processor. Toss together all ingredients and season with salt.

Each ¾-cup serving about 38 calories and less than 1 gram fat

Photo opposite, top

SPICY PINEAPPLE, APRICOT, AND JÍCAMA SALSA
Makes about 4 cups

Try this spicy topping with grilled chicken or fish.

½ small pineapple, peeled and cored
1 small red onion
1 (½-lb) piece *jícama**, peeled and cut into ¼-inch dice
3 oz dried apricots (⅓ cup), coarsely chopped
½ cup fresh cilantro, finely chopped
½ fresh *habanero* or Scotch bonnet chile*, finely chopped with seeds (wear rubber gloves)

*available at Latino markets and some specialty produce markets and supermarkets

Cut enough pineapple into ¼-inch dice to measure 1¾ cups. Chop enough onion to measure ¾ cup. Toss together all ingredients and season with salt.

Each 1-cup serving about 107 calories and less than 1 gram fat

Photo opposite, right

SAVORY DRIED CRANBERRY SAUCE
Makes about 1¼ cups

Pork chops, ham, and poultry are wonderful with this sauce.

¼   cup brown sugar
1   tablespoon cornstarch
1   cup dry white wine
½   cup chicken broth
1   teaspoon balsamic vinegar
½   cup dried cranberries
⅛   teaspoon dried tarragon, crumbled
2   teaspoons minced fresh flat-leaf parsley

GARNISH:
fresh flat-leaf parsley sprigs

Whisk together brown sugar and cornstarch in a small saucepan and add wine and broth, whisking until smooth. Add vinegar, cranberries, tarragon, and salt to taste and simmer, stirring occasionally, 15 minutes. Stir in minced parsley and simmer 1 minute more. Serve sauce hot.

Photo below

CHARRED TOMATO, CHIPOTLE, AND MANGO SALSA
Makes about 1½ cups

Try this fiery sauce with halibut steaks.

⅔   lb plum tomatoes (3 medium), quartered
1   to 2 canned *chipotle* chiles in *adobo*, seeded (wear rubber gloves)
¼   cup fresh lime juice
1   tablespoon honey, or to taste
1   ripe mango, peeled and finely chopped

Preheat broiler.

Broil tomatoes in a shallow baking pan 4 to 5 inches from heat until slightly charred, about 15 minutes. Purée tomatoes, *chipotles*, lime juice, and honey in a blender or food processor.

Stir together tomato mixture and mango and season with salt.

Each ⅓-cup serving about 68 calories and less than 1 gram fat

Photo below

ASIAN PEANUT SAUCE

Makes about 1⅔ cups

Coconut milk gives this sauce creaminess while the peanut butter provides a nutty flavor. A peppery bite comes from fresh ginger and red pepper flakes. Depending on the brand of coconut milk used, you may need to thin the sauce with a couple tablespoons of water. This sauce may be kept, covered and chilled, 5 days. Give it a try with chicken.

- ⅔ cup well-stirred canned coconut milk
- ½ cup creamy peanut butter
- 1½ tablespoons Asian fish sauce
- 1½ tablespoons soy sauce
- 1 tablespoon minced peeled fresh ginger
- 1½ teaspoons packed light brown sugar
- 1 teaspoon fresh lemon or lime juice
- ½ teaspoon dried hot red pepper flakes

Blend all ingredients in a blender or food processor until smooth.

MINT CHUTNEY WITH ORANGE AND CHILE

Makes about ¾ cup

Citrusy and minty with a hit of chile heat—this is just the right complement to lamb or pork.

- 1½ cups fresh mint
- ¼ cup finely chopped red onion
- 3 tablespoons water
- 2 tablespoons fresh lime juice
- 1 tablespoon fresh orange juice
- 1 tablespoon sugar
- 1 teaspoon freshly grated orange zest
- ¼ teaspoon kosher salt
- 1 mildly hot fresh red chile such as red jalapeño, finely chopped

Pulse all ingredients in a food processor until coarsely chopped.

CHIPOTLE YOGURT SAUCE WITH CUMIN

Makes about 1 cup

Here, chipotle chile lends smoky spicy flavor while the tang of yogurt lightens the mayonnaise. We enjoyed this sauce with beef and pork.

- 1 teaspoon cumin seeds
- ½ cup mayonnaise
- ⅓ cup plain yogurt
- ¼ cup finely chopped scallions
- 1 teaspoon minced canned *chipotle* chile in *adobo* sauce plus 1 teaspoon *adobo*

Toast cumin seeds in a small dry heavy skillet over moderate heat, shaking skillet, until 1 shade darker, about 3 minutes. Cool and finely grind with a mortar and pestle or an electric spice/coffee grinder. Stir together cumin with remaining ingredients and salt to taste in a small bowl.

QUICK SOUPS

This collection of everyday soups includes classics—borscht, gazpacho, and Chinese chicken noodle, among them—as well as more exotic creations—chicken *pozole*, pumpkin mulligatawny, and spicy shrimp and coconut milk soup with Asian noodles, to name just a few. There's a nice variety of cold and hot soups and some that can be served either way. A few, admittedly, have cream, but many are low in fat and calories. Best of all, each one is fast and easy to prepare. Add a green salad or one of our sensational sandwiches and you've got dinner, simple but hardly plain.

MUSHROOM AND LEEK SOUP

Makes about 3 cups

2   medium leeks, cut into
    ¼-inch-thick rounds
2   tablespoons unsalted butter
¾   lb mushrooms, thinly sliced
¼   cup dry white wine
1   (14½-oz) can chicken broth
1   tablespoon chopped fresh chives

Wash leeks well in a large bowl of cold water and
lift from water into a colander to drain. Heat
butter in a 3-quart saucepan over moderately
high heat until foam subsides, then sauté leeks,
stirring, 5 minutes. Add mushrooms and sauté,
stirring, until liquid mushrooms give off is
evaporated and mushrooms begin to brown.
Add wine and boil 1 minute. Add broth and
salt and pepper to taste and simmer 2 minutes.

Serve soup sprinkled with chives. Recipe may be
doubled to serve 4.

Photo on page 91

BORSCHT

Serves 4

4   medium boiling potatoes, peeled
    and halved
2   carrots, coarsely chopped
2   celery ribs, coarsely chopped
1   medium onion, chopped
1   tablespoon vegetable oil
1   (14- to 15-oz) can beef broth
1   (16-oz) jar sliced pickled beets
4   tablespoons sour cream
3   tablespoons chopped fresh dill

Cover potatoes with cold salted water by 1 inch
and simmer until tender, 20 to 25 minutes.
Drain and keep warm.

While potatoes are boiling, sauté carrots, celery,
and onion in oil in a 3-quart heavy saucepan
over high heat, stirring frequently, until beginning to brown. Add broth and bring to a boil.
Simmer, covered, until vegetables are tender,
about 13 minutes. Stir in beets and their brine
and simmer, covered, 8 minutes more. Ladle
borscht into bowls and add potatoes. Top with
sour cream and dill.

Photo opposite

CHINESE CHICKEN NOODLE SOUP

Makes about 8 cups

2   (15-oz) cans fat-free chicken broth
2   cups water
4   scallions, white parts crushed and green
    parts sliced
6   (⅛-inch thick) slices peeled fresh ginger
¼   lb carrots, thinly sliced crosswise
1   boneless skinless chicken breast (¾ lb),
    cut into 1-inch strips
1   (3-oz) package ramen noodles, broken
    into 3-inch lengths (discard seasoning packet)
2   tablespoons soy sauce
1   tablespoon Sherry
1   teaspoon rice vinegar

Bring chicken broth, water, white parts of
scallions, and ginger to a boil and simmer,
covered, 10 minutes.

Discard scallions and ginger from broth. Add
carrots and simmer 2 minutes. Add chicken and
noodles and simmer until chicken is cooked
through and noodles are tender, about 3 minutes.
Stir in soy sauce, Sherry, vinegar, and remaining
scallions and bring to a boil. Remove from heat
and serve immediately.

Each serving about 135 calories and
less than 1 gram fat

CRAB CHOWDER
Makes about 4 cups

If you prefer your soup a little thicker, crush 6 saltines into fine crumbs and add them at the end of the procedure, when you add the crab.

2 bacon slices, chopped
1 medium onion, cut into ¼-inch dice
2 medium boiling potatoes, peeled and
   cut into ¼-inch dice
½ cup water
3 cups whole milk
⅛ teaspoon cayenne, or to taste
½ lb jumbo lump crab meat,
   picked over

GARNISH:
chopped fresh flat-leaf parsley

Cook bacon in a 2-quart heavy saucepan over moderate heat, stirring occasionally, until crisp. Transfer with a slotted spoon to paper towels to drain, reserving fat in pan.

Stir onion, potatoes, and water into reserved fat and simmer, covered, until potatoes are tender and most of water is evaporated, about 15 minutes.

Stir milk and cayenne into mixture and return just to a simmer. Add crab and salt and pepper to taste and bring chowder to a simmer.

Serve chowder sprinkled with bacon.

Photo left, top

PLANTAIN SOUP

Makes about 8 cups

6 cups chicken broth
3 semi-ripe (yellow with some spots) plantains*, trimmed, peeled, and cut into ½-inch-thick slices
1 large carrot, grated
1 teaspoon ground cumin

available at Latino markets and many specialty produce markets and supermarkets

Bring broth to a boil in a 4-quart heavy saucepan with plantains, carrot, and cumin. Simmer, covered, until plantains are very tender, 20 to 25 minutes.

Purée mixture in batches in a blender (use caution when blending hot liquids) and season with salt and pepper.

Photo opposite, bottom

LENTIL SOUP WITH SPINACH AND TOMATO

Makes about 9 cups

½ cup lentils
4 cups water
½ lb onions, finely chopped
2 teaspoons minced garlic
1 tablespoon olive oil
1 teaspoon curry powder
2 (15-oz) cans fat-free chicken or vegetable broth
2 cups canned crushed tomatoes
1 (10-oz) package frozen chopped spinach
1 teaspoon sugar
¼ cup chopped parsley
1 teaspoon red-wine vinegar

Simmer lentils in water in a 5-quart pot, covered, until tender, about 20 minutes.

While lentils are cooking, cook onions and 1½ teaspoons garlic in oil in a large nonstick skillet over moderate heat, stirring, until tender and golden. Stir in curry powder and cook 1 minute.

Add broth, tomatoes, spinach, sugar, and onion mixture to lentils and simmer 10 minutes. Stir in parsley, vinegar, and remaining garlic and bring to a boil. Remove from heat and season with salt and pepper.

Each serving about 143 calories and 3 grams fat

WHITE BEAN, SAUSAGE, AND ESCAROLE SOUP

Makes about 9 cups

1 lb sweet Italian sausage
1 tablespoon olive oil
1 head escarole (1 lb), chopped
2 large garlic cloves, chopped
2 (15-oz) cans chicken broth
2 cups water
2 (19-oz) cans *cannellini* beans, rinsed and drained
½ cup freshly grated parmesan

Squeeze sausage from casings into a 5-quart heavy pot and cook in oil over moderate heat, stirring to break up large lumps, until golden. Pour off all but 1 tablespoon drippings.

Stir in escarole and garlic and sauté over moderately high heat until escarole is wilted. Add chicken broth and water and simmer 5 minutes.

Mash half of *cannellini* beans with a potato masher or fork. Add all beans to mixture and simmer 5 minutes. Stir in cheese and season with salt and pepper.

HOW TO QUICKLY
CHILL SOUPS

So how do our cooks recommend
that we cool soups quickly?
There are two ways, essentially.
The first involves placing a large bowl
or pot of soup into a larger container
of ice water and stirring the soup
until it cools.

Alternatively, if you're low on ice
(and have a large freezer with room
to spare), you can transfer the soup
to a shallow container and put it in
the freezer, removing every few
minutes and stirring until cool.

Either method produces refreshingly
delicious chilled soup in minutes.

—Ellen Morrissey

CHILLED ZUCCHINI
HERB SOUP
Makes about 6 cups

If preferred, this soup may be served hot.

1½   lb zucchini, cut into 1-inch pieces
4   cups fat-free chicken or vegetable broth
½   lb onions, chopped
1   tablespoon olive oil
½   cup fresh flat-leaf parsley
½   cup fresh basil
¼   cup chopped fresh chives
½   to 1 teaspoon chopped garlic
½   cup cold water

Simmer zucchini in broth in a 3-quart saucepan
until tender, about 10 minutes.

While zucchini is simmering, sauté onions in
oil with salt to taste in a nonstick skillet over
moderately high heat, stirring occasionally,
until softened but not browned.

Purée zucchini mixture, onion mixture, parsley,
basil, chives, and garlic in batches in a blender
(use caution when blending hot liquids). Season
with salt and pepper. Transfer soup to a metal
bowl and stir in water. Set bowl in a larger bowl
of ice and cold water and stir soup until chilled.

Each serving about 69 calories and 4 grams fat

CHILLED PEA SOUP WITH TARRAGON

Serves 2 (makes about 3½ cups)

This soup is also delicious served hot.

½ cup sliced shallots
1½ tablespoons olive oil
1 (15-oz) can chicken broth
1 (10-oz) package frozen baby peas
1½ tablespoons coarsely chopped fresh tarragon
½ teaspoon sugar
¼ cup heavy cream
1 teaspoon fresh lemon juice

Cook shallots in oil in a 3-quart saucepan over moderate heat until tender but not browned. Add chicken broth and peas and simmer, covered, 5 minutes. Purée in a blender with remaining ingredients and salt to taste (use caution when blending hot liquids) and pour through a fine sieve into a metal bowl.

Set bowl in a larger bowl of ice and cold water and stir soup until chilled.

MISO SOUP

Serves 2 (makes about 2½ cups)

1 (15-oz) can chicken broth
½ cup water
2 tablespoons *shiro miso* (white fermented-soybean paste)*
4 shiitake mushrooms, stems discarded and caps thinly sliced
6 snow peas, thinly sliced diagonally
¼ lb firm tofu, cut into ½-inch cubes
¼ cup baby spinach, coarse stems discarded
1 tablespoon soy sauce
1 teaspoon *sake*
½ teaspoon rice vinegar

*available at health food stores and Asian markets

Simmer broth, water, *miso*, and shiitakes, stirring to dissolve *miso*, until mushrooms are tender, about 3 minutes. Stir in peas, tofu, and spinach and simmer 1 minute. Stir in soy sauce, *sake*, and vinegar and bring to a boil. Remove from heat and serve immediately.

PUMPKIN MULLIGATAWNY SOUP

Makes about 5 cups

¾ lb onions, chopped
2 tablespoons vegetable oil
2 teaspoons curry powder
1 tablespoon ground coriander
1 teaspoon ground cumin
1 (15-oz) can pumpkin purée
2 cups milk
1 tablespoon Major Grey's chutney or apricot preserves
1 cup water
1 cup heavy cream
2 tablespoons fresh lemon juice

Cook onion in oil in a 4-quart saucepan over moderate heat, stirring occasionally, until softened and pale golden. Add curry powder, coriander, and cumin and cook, stirring, 1 minute.

Purée onion mixture, pumpkin, milk, and chutney in a blender. Return to saucepan and stir in water, cream, lemon juice, and salt and pepper to taste. Simmer, covered, 10 minutes.

CHILLED CORN SOUP WITH CHILE PURÉE

Makes about 7 cups

For a super-quick—and equally delicious—soup, omit the chile purée. This dish also may be served hot.

8   cups fresh corn kernels (from 10 to 14 ears)
6   cups water plus additional for thinning (if necessary)
1   tablespoon kosher salt
    For chile purée
1   large mild dried chile, such as *guajillo*, *pasilla*, or *ancho* (including seeds), cut into 1-inch pieces
1   small onion, sliced
1   tablespoon olive oil
½   teaspoon ground cumin
½   cup water plus additional for thinning (if necessary)

¼   cup snipped fresh chives

Simmer corn kernels in water with salt, covered, 20 minutes, or until very tender.

Make chile purée:
While corn is simmering, cook chile and onion in oil in a small saucepan over moderate heat until onion is tender. Stir in cumin and cook, stirring, 1 minute. Add ½ cup water and simmer until chile is tender, about 5 minutes. Purée mixture in a blender (use caution when blending hot liquids) and season with salt. (If purée is too thick, add additional water to thin to desired consistency.)

Purée corn soup in batches in clean blender (use caution when blending hot liquids). Pour through a sieve into a metal bowl. Set bowl in a larger bowl of ice and cold water and stir soup until chilled. (If soup is too thick, add additional water to thin to desired consistency.)

Serve corn soup drizzled with chile purée and sprinkled with chives.

CHICKEN POZOLE SOUP

Makes about 8 cups

½   lb onions, chopped
2   dried *ancho* chiles, 1 seeded and both cut into 1-inch pieces
2   tablespoons olive oil
¾   teaspoon ground cumin
½   teaspoon dried oregano, crumbled
2   (15-oz) cans chicken broth
2   cups water
4   chicken thighs (1¼ lb)
1   (1 lb 13-oz) can white hominy (*pozole*), drained
½   cup chopped cilantro

Sauté onion and chiles in oil in a 4- to 5-quart saucepan over moderately high heat, stirring, until onions are tender and golden. Add cumin and oregano and cook, stirring, 1 minute. Add chicken broth, water, and chicken thighs and simmer, covered, 20 minutes.

Remove thighs from broth and cool slightly. Purée broth mixture in 2 batches in a blender until very smooth (use caution when blending hot liquids), and return to saucepan. Cut meat from thighs and stir into soup with hominy. Simmer 5 minutes. Stir in cilantro and season with salt.

WHICH WAY TO PURÉE?

Glorious homemade soups come in a number of forms, and many require puréeing. This, as you probably know, can be achieved in several ways, but what you may not know is that different equipment produces different results. Which equipment should you choose? Here are your options:

The **blender** is the machine preferred by most *Gourmet* food editors for achieving velvety smooth purées—a few swirls of the blade and *voila*! (In England, blenders are called "liquidizers," a more descriptive name for the work they actually do.) **Food processors** function in much the same way, although the resulting purées may not be quite as silky. Whichever appliance you choose, be sure to use caution when puréeing hot liquids, as they can scald you. It's a good idea to let hot soup cool for five minutes or so before putting it in the machine, and to fill the container only half way. Also, some blenders have lids with a removable inner section that should be opened to allow steam to escape; the food processor's feed tube should also be left open when puréeing anything hot.

Hand-held immersion blenders, although not as powerful as food processors or standing blenders, allow for very quick and easy puréeing directly in the soup pot. When finished, simply disengage the small attachment and clean. A few of the more inexpensive models may lack the motor strength to purée thoroughly, resulting in soups that are somewhat rough in texture. Should you want a smoother soup, push the mixture through a sieve to remove any lingering skins, seeds, or large chunks.

A **food mill** might seem old-fashioned, but it produces peel-, pulp-, and seed-free soup. The various sized discs allow you to control just how smooth you want your purée, without the extra step of straining.

—Ellen Morrissey

SPICY SHRIMP AND COCONUT MILK SOUP WITH ASIAN NOODLES

Makes about 8 cups

- 6 oz bean-thread or thin rice stick noodles
- 1 tablespoon minced garlic
- 1 tablespoon grated peeled fresh ginger
- 1 tablespoon minced shallot
- 1 large jalapeño (half of seeds discarded), minced
- 2 tablespoons vegetable oil
- 1 (19-oz) can unsweetened coconut milk
- 4 cups water
- ½ lb shelled large shrimp, halved lengthwise
- 1 cup fresh bean sprouts, threadlike tails discarded
- 2 tablespoons Asian fish sauce
- 1 tablespoon fresh lime juice
- 1 cup chopped fresh cilantro

GARNISHES:
lime wedges and cilantro sprigs

Soak noodles in hot tap water to cover 15 minutes. Cut into 3-inch lengths with scissors.

Sauté garlic, ginger, shallot, and jalapeño in oil in a 5-quart pot until fragrant. Stir in coconut milk and water and bring to a boil. Stir in shrimp and noodles and simmer 1 minute. Stir in remaining ingredients and bring to a boil. Remove from heat and serve immediately.

QUICK GAZPACHO WITH PARSLEY PESTO

Makes about 6 cups

On a warm summer's day there is nothing like chilled gazpacho. To speed up the chilling time, keep canned tomatoes in the refrigerator until you make this dish.

FOR GAZPACHO
- 1 (12-oz) bottle roasted red peppers, drained
- 1 (35-oz) can fine-quality Italian-style peeled whole tomatoes with liquid
- 1 cup coarsely chopped cucumber
- ½ cup coarsely chopped white onion
- ¼ cup extra-virgin olive oil
- 1½ tablespoons red-wine vinegar
- ½ teaspoon sugar
- ½ cup water for thinning soup, if necessary

FOR PESTO
- 1 cup flat-leaf parsley
- ¼ cup extra-virgin olive oil
- ¼ cup water
- 1 garlic clove
- ½ teaspoon salt

MAKE GAZPACHO:
Purée roasted peppers in a blender. Add tomatoes, cucumber, onion, oil, vinegar, and sugar and pulse until vegetables are finely chopped. Season with salt and pepper and chill. (If soup is too thick, add additional water, 2 tablespoons at a time, to thin to desired consistency.)

MAKE PESTO:
Purée pesto ingredients in clean blender.

Serve gazpacho chilled or at room temperature, drizzled with pesto.

BARLEY VEGETABLE SOUP

Makes about 7 cups

- ½ lb onions, chopped
- ¾ lb mushrooms, cut into ¼-inch-thick slices
- 2 tablespoons olive oil
- ½ lb carrots, cut into ¼-inch-thick slices
- 1 celery rib, chopped
- ½ cup barley
- 8 cups water
- ½ cup chopped flat-leaf parsley
- 2 tablespoons soy sauce

Sauté onions, mushrooms, and salt to taste in oil in a 4-quart heavy saucepan over moderately high heat until any liquid mushrooms give off evaporates and vegetables are golden, about 10 minutes. Add carrots, celery, barley, and water and simmer 25 minutes. Stir in parsley and soy sauce and cook 5 minutes. Season with salt.

RED LENTIL AND CARROT SOUP

Makes about 8 cups

- ¾ lb red lentils*, picked over
- 7 cups water
- 1 cup chopped onion
- 3 garlic cloves, minced
- 1 teaspoon ground coriander
- 1 teaspoon ground cumin
- ¼ teaspoon turmeric
- 5 carrots (10 oz), halved lengthwise and thinly sliced crosswise
- 1 cup finely chopped red bell pepper
- ¼ cup fresh cilantro, finely chopped
- ¼ cup chopped scallion greens
   Cayenne to taste

GARNISH:
fresh cilantro sprigs

*available at natural foods stores and specialty foods shops

Bring lentils and water to a boil in a 4-quart saucepan and skim froth. Stir in onion, garlic, coriander, cumin, and turmeric and simmer, partially covered, 15 minutes. Stir in carrots and bell pepper and simmer until carrots are tender, about 10 minutes. Stir in cilantro, scallion, cayenne, and salt and pepper to taste.

Each serving about 339 calories and less than 1 gram fat

Photo left

QUICK sandwiches and burgers

Why make an ordinary grilled cheese sandwich when you can have grilled Cheddar and bacon on raisin bread?; a turkey on rye, when you can have smoked turkey, bell pepper, mango, and *chipotle* mayo wrapped in *lavash*?; or a plain old burger, when you can have a guacamole cheeseburger, or an herbed turkey burger, or hey, why not an Asian salmon burger with pickled cucumber on pumpernickel? Delve into the following chapter, and you'll surely recognize many of your old favorites all dressed up in exciting new combinations. Today's supermarkets are bursting at the seams with plenty of unusual breads and condiments. Here's your chance to give them a try.

CURRIED CHICKEN AND MANGO SANDWICHES
Makes 2 sandwiches

We particularly liked this sandwich on slipper-shaped ciabatta bread, although any type of soft Italian bread is suitable.

- ¼ cup mayonnaise
- 1 tablespoon sour cream
- 1½ teaspoons chopped fresh cilantro
- 1 teaspoon curry powder
- 2 skinless boneless chicken breast halves (¾ lb total)
- 1 teaspoon olive oil
- 1 (7-inch) length of soft Italian bread such as *ciabatta*
- 4 small soft-leafed lettuce leaves
- ½ firm-ripe mango, peeled and thinly sliced lengthwise

Stir together mayonnaise, sour cream, cilantro, curry powder, and salt and pepper to taste.

Pat chicken dry and season with salt and pepper. Heat oil in a 9-inch nonstick skillet over moderately high heat until hot but not smoking, then sauté chicken 4 minutes on each side, or until cooked through. Transfer to a cutting board and let stand 5 minutes. Diagonally slice chicken and season with salt and pepper.

Halve bread horizontally with a serrated knife and spread cut sides with mayonnaise mixture. Make sandwiches with chicken, lettuce, and mango and cut in half.

Photo on page 103

CRAB MELT SANDWICHES
Makes 4 open-face sandwiches

- 1 lb fresh jumbo lump crab meat, picked over
- 2 tablespoons fresh lime juice, or to taste
- ½ cup mayonnaise
- 2 teaspoons Creole or other coarse-grained mustard
- 4 (1-inch-thick) slices brioche or challah
  Unsalted butter, softened (optional)
- 4 tablespoons freshly grated parmesan

GARNISHES:
chopped fresh chives and lime wedges

Toss together crab meat (do not shred) and 1 tablespoon lime juice in a bowl.

Whisk together remaining tablespoon lime juice, mayonnaise, and mustard. Pour sauce over crab and toss to coat. Season with salt and pepper and chill, covered, 30 minutes.

Preheat broiler.

Lightly toast bread and with a 3¼-inch round cutter cut out rounds. Lightly butter toast, if desired. Spoon one fourth crab mixture into a ½-cup measure. Holding a toast round on top of mixture in measure, invert crab onto round and set on an ungreased baking sheet. Repeat with remaining crab mixture and rounds and sprinkle 1 tablespoon parmesan over each sandwich. Broil about 3 inches from heat until cheese is melted and golden, 1 to 2 minutes.

Photo opposite, top

WARM GOAT CHEESE, BEET, AND ARUGULA SANDWICHES

Makes 4 sandwiches

2	teaspoons balsamic vinegar
½	teaspoon Dijon mustard
3	tablespoons olive oil
1	(14- to 15-oz) can sliced beets, drained
8	(½-inch-thick) bread slices from a round country loaf
6	oz soft mild goat cheese, softened
4	very thin slices red onion, rings separated
16	large arugula leaves

Preheat broiler.

Whisk together vinegar, mustard, and salt and pepper to taste, then whisk in 2 tablespoons oil. Toss beets with vinaigrette.

Arrange bread on a large baking sheet and brush with remaining tablespoon oil. Season with salt and pepper and broil 6 inches from heat 1 to 1½ minutes, or until edges are golden. Remove 4 slices from oven. Turn remaining 4 slices over on baking sheet and spread thickly with goat cheese. Broil 1 minute more and transfer to plates. Top goat cheese with drained beets, onion, arugula, and remaining bread, toasted sides up.

Photo left, bottom

GRILLED CHEDDAR AND BACON ON RAISIN BREAD

Makes 4 sandwiches

3   tablespoons unsalted butter,
     softened
8   slices raisin bread
½   lb thinly sliced extra-sharp Cheddar
8   bacon slices, cooked until crisp and
     drained on paper towels

Butter one side of each raisin bread slice on a
large sheet of wax paper and turn slices over.
Arrange Cheddar on unbuttered sides of bread
and top 4 slices with bacon. Flip remaining
bread onto bacon.

Heat a nonstick skillet over moderate heat until
hot and cook sandwiches in batches, pressing
lightly with a metal spatula, until undersides are
golden, about 1 minute. Turn sandwiches over
and cook, pressing lightly, until undersides are
golden and cheese is melted, about 1 minute.

Photo below

PEANUT BUTTER, APPLE, AND BACON SANDWICHES

Makes 2 sandwiches

½   cup creamy or chunky peanut butter
4   large slices whole-wheat bread,
     lightly toasted
8   bacon slices, cooked until crisp and
     drained on paper towels
1   small crisp apple such as Royal Gala,
     cored and thinly sliced
½   cup alfalfa sprouts

Spread peanut butter evenly on bread slices.
Make sandwiches with bread, bacon, apple slices,
and sprouts.

Photo below

SMOKED TURKEY, MANGO, AND CHIPOTLE MAYO WRAPS

Serves 4

¼ cup low-fat mayonnaise
¾ teaspoon finely chopped *chipotle* chile in *adobo* plus ¼ teaspoon *adobo* sauce, or to taste
1 (13-inch) very thin pliable round *lavash**, quartered
¼ lb sliced smoked turkey
½ mango, peeled, pitted, and cut into julienne strips
1 (4-oz) bottle roasted red bell peppers, rinsed, drained, and cut into strips

*available at Middle Eastern markets, specialty foods shops, and some supermarkets

Stir together mayonnaise, *chipotle* chile, *adobo* sauce, and salt and pepper to taste.

Spread 1 side of each *lavash* quarter evenly with some *chipotle* mayonnaise, leaving a ½-inch border all around, then top with 1 layer of turkey. Season with salt and pepper. Top turkey with mango and roasted peppers and tightly roll up each *lavash* quarter into a cone.

Wrap individually in wax paper.

Each wrap about 171 calories and 6 grams fat

CHIPOTLE CHILES

Their name is from the Aztec *chilli poctli*, "smoked chile," and tips you off as to their preparation. When cherry-red ripe jalapeños are smoked and dried, they are called *chipotles* (chi-*pote*-lays). The ripeness of their former incarnation helps explain the sweetness underneath the savor, and the smokiness mellows the heat. *Chipotles* canned in the tomato-based sauce called *adobo* take the flavor in a different, more piquant direction. Both kinds of *chipotles* are available at Latino markets, specialty foods shops, and some supermarkets. (The dried ones are usually wrapped in cellophane and hanging in the produce department.) They can also be ordered from Chile Today–Hot Tamale, Inc., (800) 468-7377. Sweet, smoky, hot. What else could you possibly want?

—Jane Daniels Lear

TURKEY AND BLACK-BEAN SALSA TORTILLA ROLLS

Makes 4 tortilla rolls

½ cup canned black beans, rinsed and drained
1 large vine-ripened tomato, seeded and chopped
2 pickled jalapeños, seeded and chopped (wear rubber gloves)
4 teaspoons fresh lime juice
½ teaspoon chili powder
½ ripe California avocado
2 tablespoons low-fat plain yogurt
4 (10-inch) whole-wheat tortillas*
½ lb thinly sliced roast turkey breast
1 cup fresh cilantro, coarsely chopped

available at Hispanic markets, some supermarkets, and by mail order from Maria & Ricardo's Tortilla Factory, 30 Germania Street, Jamaica Plain, MA 02130, (617) 524-6107

Stir together black beans, tomato, jalapeños, 2 teaspoons lime juice, chili powder, and salt to taste.

Purée avocado, yogurt, remaining 2 teaspoons lime juice, and salt to taste in a food processor. (Alternatively, mash avocado mixture with a fork until smooth.)

Spread avocado mixture evenly on tortillas and arrange turkey across each tortilla just below middle. Top with black bean salsa and cilantro and roll up tortillas tightly, leaving ends open. Halve diagonally with a serrated knife.

Each serving about 297 calories and 10 grams fat

Photo right, top

BROILED CHICKEN AND ROASTED PEPPER SANDWICHES

Makes 2 sandwiches

½   lb Parmigiano-Reggiano
2   skinless boneless chicken breast halves
1   tablespoon balsamic vinegar
4   tablespoons olive oil
1   round loaf crusty bread (8 inches in diameter)
1   large garlic clove, halved crosswise
1   large red or yellow bell pepper, roasted, peeled, and cut into 1-inch-wide strips (procedure on page 127)
¼   cup fresh basil

Preheat broiler.

Shave enough cheese with a vegetable peeler to measure about ½ cup.

Put chicken between 2 sheets of dampened plastic wrap and lightly pound with a rolling pin or flat side of a meat pounder to about ¼ inch thick. Arrange on lightly oiled rack of a broiler pan.

Whisk together vinegar, 1 tablespoon oil, and salt and pepper to taste. Brush chicken with some vinaigrette and broil 2 to 3 inches from heat 5 minutes. Turn chicken over and brush with some remaining vinaigrette. Broil until just cooked through, about 5 minutes more. Transfer chicken to a plate and keep warm, loosely covered with foil.

Cut four ½-inch-thick slices from middle of loaf and lightly brush both sides of each slice with remaining 3 tablespoons oil. Toast bread on broiler pan under broiler. Rub garlic over 1 side of each slice of toast.

Make sandwiches with chicken, peppers, cheese shavings, and basil and season with salt and pepper.

Photo opposite, bottom

TURKEY-WATERCRESS CLUB SANDWICHES

Makes 4 sandwiches

1   tablespoon olive oil
2   tablespoons fresh lemon juice
¾   teaspoon freshly ground black pepper
1   garlic clove, minced
¾   lb turkey cutlets (each ⅓ inch thick)
¾   cup watercress leaves plus 1 cup tender sprigs
⅓   cup mayonnaise
12   (½-inch) slices brioche or challah, toasted
12   bacon slices, cooked until crisp and drained
3   small tomatoes, sliced

Whisk together oil, 1 tablespoon lemon juice, pepper, and garlic in a shallow dish and add turkey. Marinate turkey, turning once, 30 minutes. Discard marinade. Heat a well-seasoned ridged grill pan over moderately high heat until hot, then grill turkey 3 minutes on each side, or until just cooked through. Cool on a cutting board and cut into 4 portions.

Purée watercress leaves and mayonnaise in a food processor or blender and blend in remaining tablespoon lemon juice and salt and pepper to taste.

Spread watercress mayonnaise on 8 toast slices and top 4 with turkey and salt and pepper to taste. Top turkey with 4 remaining mayonnaise-spread toasts, mayonnaise sides up, and top each portion with bacon, tomatoes, and watercress sprigs. Top with remaining toasts.

Photo below

ASIAN SALMON BURGERS WITH PICKLED CUCUMBER ON PUMPERNICKEL

Makes 4 burgers

Note: To slice the cucumber into a paper-thin spiral, we used a Japanese rotary device known as the Benriner vegetable slicer. This gadget is available from Katagiri, 224 East 59th Street, New York, NY 10022, (212) 755-3566 and through the Williams-Sonoma catalogue, (800) 541-2233 (ask for the "spiral shredder").

1	large cucumber (1 lb)
1	tablespoon cider vinegar
1½	teaspoons sugar
¼	teaspoon dried hot red pepper flakes
1	large egg white
1	tablespoon soy sauce
½	teaspoon grated peeled fresh ginger
1	(¾-lb) piece salmon fillet, skin discarded and fish cut into ¼-inch pieces
½	cup fine fresh bread crumbs
2	scallions, finely chopped
1	teaspoon mustard seeds
1	teaspoon vegetable oil
4	small green lettuce leaves
8	firm pumpernickel slices (10 oz total)

Cut cucumber into 1 long spiral with a Japanese rotary slicer. (Alternatively, cut cucumber into very thin slices with a sharp knife.) Toss cucumber with vinegar, sugar, red pepper flakes, and salt to taste in a bowl.

Whisk together egg white, soy sauce, and ginger in another bowl and stir in salmon, bread crumbs, scallions, mustard seeds, and salt to taste. Purée ⅓ cup salmon mixture in a food processor and return to salmon mixture remaining in bowl. (Alternatively, chop ⅓ cup salmon mixture fine and mash to a paste with flat side of a knife.) Stir mixture to combine and form into four ¾-inch-thick patties. Drain cucumber well.

Heat vegetable oil in a large nonstick skillet over moderately high heat until hot but not smoking, then cook patties until golden, about 2 minutes on each side. Cook patties, covered, over moderate heat until just cooked through, about 5 minutes more. Make burgers with lettuce leaves, pumpernickel slices, and pickled cucumber.

Each sandwich about 322 calories and 8 grams fat

Photo opposite

HUMMUS, CARROT, AND CUCUMBER LAVASH WRAPS

Makes 4

1	cup drained canned chickpeas, rinsed
1	garlic clove, minced
1½	tablespoons fresh lemon juice
2	teaspoons extra-virgin olive oil
¼	teaspoon dark Asian sesame oil
3	tablespoons finely chopped fresh cilantro
1	(13-inch) very thin pliable round *lavash**, quartered
2	carrots, coarsely grated
¼	seedless cucumber, seeded and cut into julienne strips
⅓	cup alfalfa sprouts

**available at Middle Eastern markets, specialty foods shops, and some supermarkets*

Purée chickpeas, garlic, lemon juice, oils, and salt and pepper to taste in a food processor. Transfer to a bowl and stir in cilantro.

Spread 1 side of each *lavash* quarter evenly with some hummus, leaving a ½-inch border all around, then top with some vegetables and sprouts. Season with salt and pepper and tightly roll up each *lavash* quarter into a cone. Wrap individually in wax paper.

Each wrap about 159 calories and 3 grams fat

COOKING CLASS: Burgers

Ground meat is treated with suspicion these days, and there is reason enough to be leery. If you are cooking for a child, an elderly person, or anyone with a compromised immune system, you must not take chances; any burgers you serve them should look like the sample at right, which is cooked to 160°F and deemed safe by the USDA. Those of us who prefer a rosy hamburger, though, like the one at left, assume a certain element of risk. I am encouraged by the odds—more than 30 percent of all U.S. citizens have consumed ground beef in some form within the past 24 hours.

Whether my burgers are basic or embellished, if I can't find either antibiotic- and hormone-free beef or my new favorite, buffalo—which, so far, only comes that way—I'll rethink dinner. I preferred, until recently, ground chuck with 15 to 20 percent fat. Then I discovered Coleman's chuck, the one that's 90 percent lean. Delicious. I shy away from ground sirloin, though; it's both expensive and bland. At the other end of the spectrum, I have always eschewed anything labeled simply "ground beef" because of its strong flavor and vague nomenclature.

Another key to a great burger is the way it is formed. I generally allow about six ounces of meat per person, or three burgers to a pound. The best way to portion the meat without overhandling it is to cut it crosswise into three squarish lumps, then gently pat each lump into a patty about an inch thick.

To cook, I haul out my cherished cast-iron ridged grill pan and preheat it for about three minutes over a medium flame. Then I lavishly season both sides of the patties with coarse salt and black pepper and cook them about four minutes on each side for medium-rare. Don't make the mistake of pressing the patties down with a spatula—you'll lose lots of lovely juice that way. One last point: I treat a burger as I would a steak and let it rest after cooking; a minute or so is fine. I flip it over halfway through so the juices get evenly distributed. This is no road burger, flat and highway gray; this is homemade joy, home-made rapture.

—Zanne Stewart

GUACAMOLE CHEESEBURGERS

Makes 3 burgers

- 1 firm-ripe avocado (preferably California), halved, pitted, and peeled
- 2 teaspoons fresh lemon juice
- 1 plum tomato, seeded and chopped
- ¼ cup thinly sliced scallion
- 1 tablespoon minced fresh cilantro, or to taste
- 1 lb ground beef (preferably naturally raised)
- ¼ lb sharp Cheddar, very thinly sliced
- 6 large oval slices pumpernickel
- 2 radishes, thinly sliced

GARNISH:
whole radishes

Mash one-fourth of avocado with a fork in a bowl. Add lemon juice and salt to taste and mash until smooth. Stir in tomato, scallion, and cilantro. Cut remaining avocado into ¼-inch dice and stir into mixture. Fold guacamole together gently but thoroughly. Cover surface of guacamole with wax paper and reserve.

Handling beef as little as possible, divide into thirds and shape into ovals. Season generously with salt and pepper. Heat a well-seasoned ridged grill pan (preferably cast-iron) over moderately high heat until hot, then cook hamburgers 5½ minutes on each side for rare. Top hamburgers with cheese and cook, covered, 1 minute. Transfer to a plate and let stand, covered loosely, 3 minutes.

Make burgers with pumpernickel slices, guacamole, and radish slices.

Photo right

HERBED TURKEY BURGERS

Makes 7 burgers

- 1½ lb lean ground turkey
- ½ cup finely chopped fresh cilantro
- 1 large red bell pepper, finely chopped
- 1 medium onion, finely chopped
- 2 tablespoons Worcestershire sauce
- 2 teaspoons ground cumin
- ½ teaspoon Tabasco
- 7 non-fat or low-fat hamburger buns

ACCOMPANIMENTS:
alfalfa sprouts, pickles, ketchup, and mustard

Prepare grill.

Mix together turkey, cilantro, bell pepper, onion, Worcestershire, cumin, Tabasco, and salt and pepper to taste until combined well. Form into ½-inch-thick patties and grill on a lightly oiled rack set 5 to 6 inches over glowing coals 4 to 5 minutes on each side, or until just cooked through. (Alternatively, burgers can be cooked, in batches, in a well-seasoned ridged grill pan.)

Serve burgers on buns.

Each burger (not including accompaniments) about 239 calories and 8 grams fat

REFRIED BEAN AND HOT PEPPER JACK QUESADILLAS WITH PICKLED ONION

Makes 2 quesadillas

4   tablespoons olive oil
1   medium onion, chopped
¾   teaspoon ground cumin
1   cup canned pinto beans,
    rinsed and drained
¼   cup water
4   (6- to 7-inch) flour tortillas
1   cup coarsely grated Monterey Jack
    cheese with hot peppers
    Pickled onion (recipe follows)
8   fresh cilantro sprigs

Preheat oven to 500°F.

Heat 2 tablespoons oil in a heavy skillet over mod-erately high heat until hot but not smoking, then sauté chopped onion with salt to taste until soft-ened and golden. Add cumin and cook, stirring, 1 minute. Add beans and water and cook, stirring and mashing, until beans are coarsely mashed, about 5 minutes. Season with salt and pepper.

Put 2 tortillas on a baking sheet and brush with some remaining oil. Turn tortillas over and top each with half of bean mixture and ⅓ cup Monterey Jack, spreading evenly. Cover with remaining 2 tortillas and brush tops of quesadillas with remaining oil.

Bake quesadillas in middle of oven until golden, 8 to 10 minutes. Sprinkle quesadillas with remain-ing ⅓ cup Monterey Jack and bake until cheese is melted, about 1 minute. Transfer to a cutting board and cut into wedges.

Top wedges with pickled onion and cilantro.

Photo opposite, top

PICKLED ONION

½   medium red onion, cut into
    ¼-inch-thick wedges
½   cup cider vinegar
1   teaspoon pickling spices
½   teaspoon salt

Simmer all ingredients in a small saucepan 2 minutes and transfer to a bowl. Chill onion, covered.

FETA AND WALNUT QUESADILLAS WITH APPLE-FIG SALSA

Makes 2 quesadillas

½   Granny Smith apple, cut into ¼-inch dice
¼   cup diced dried Calimyrna figs
1   tablespoon fresh lemon juice
1   tablespoon chopped fresh flat-leaf parsley
1   teaspoon minced fresh rosemary
1   tablespoon plus 1 teaspoon honey
4   (6- to 7-inch) flour tortillas
2   tablespoons olive oil
½   cup walnuts, toasted and chopped
⅓   cup crumbled feta

Preheat oven to 500°F.

Stir together apple, figs, lemon juice, parsley, rosemary, and 1 teaspoon honey. Put 2 tortillas on a baking sheet and brush with some oil. Turn tortillas over and brush with remaining tablespoon honey. Sprinkle tortillas with walnuts and feta and cover with remaining 2 tortillas, pressing gently. Brush tops of quesadillas with remaining oil.

Bake in middle of oven until golden, 8 to 10 minutes. Transfer to a cutting board and cut into wedges.

Spoon apple-fig salsa over wedges.

Photo opposite, middle

RIPE OLIVE AND AVOCADO QUESADILLAS

Makes 2 quesadillas

1   (6-oz) can pitted ripe black olives (1⅓ cups),
    drained well and cut crosswise
    into ⅛-inch-thick slices
1   firm-ripe California avocado, halved, pitted,
    peeled, and finely chopped
1   small red bell pepper, finely chopped
⅓   cup chopped fresh cilantro
2   tablespoons finely chopped red onion
1½ tablespoons fresh lime juice
4   (6- to 7-inch) flour tortillas
½   teaspoon vegetable oil
1⅓ cups grated pepper Jack cheese (5 oz)

Stir together olives, avocado, bell pepper,
cilantro, onion, and lime juice.

Preheat broiler.

Put tortillas on a large baking sheet and brush
tops with oil. Broil tortillas 2 to 4 inches from
heat until pale golden, about 45 seconds. Turn
tortillas over and broil until pale golden. Sprinkle
tortillas evenly with cheese and broil until melted
and bubbling, about 30 seconds. Divide olive
mixture among tortillas and cut each tortilla into
4 wedges.

Photo left, bottom

QUICK PASTAS AND PIZZAS

There's no doubt about it, pasta is a great solution for the harried cook. The problem arises, however, when we continuously settle for spaghetti tossed with whatever we have on hand. What's wrong with that? Nothing really. It's just that *gemelli*, *orzo*, *soba* noodles, or, perhaps *malfada* tossed with the likes of *olivada* and roasted red peppers, tomatillo sauce, or pumpkin seed pesto may not have crossed your mind. As you'll soon discover, over a dozen enticing combinations have crossed ours. And because we believe that our beloved pizza can taste even better when it's homemade, we've created several gems—like pesto eggplant pizza and broccoli rabe pizza— that reinvent this favorite, too.

LINGUINE WITH TOMATO-BASIL CLAM SAUCE

Serves 4

1   lb plum tomatoes
3   dozen littleneck clams, cleaned
¼   cup water
½   lb dried linguine
3   garlic cloves, minced
1   tablespoon extra-virgin olive oil
½   teaspoon dried hot red pepper flakes
½   cup fresh basil, chopped

Have ready a bowl of ice and cold water. Blanch tomatoes, 2 or 3 at a time, in a saucepan of boiling water 10 seconds and transfer to ice water. Peel, seed, and dice tomatoes.

Steam clams in water in a large heavy pot, covered, over moderately high heat 5 to 10 minutes, checking after 5 minutes and transferring as they open to a bowl. (Discard any unopened clams.) Remove pot from heat, reserving cooking liquid.

Cook linguine in a 6-quart pot of boiling salted water until al dente and drain.

While linguine is cooking, remove meat from the largest 24 clams with a small knife, discarding shells, and pulse in a food processor just until coarsely chopped. Stir chopped clams, tomatoes, garlic, oil, and red pepper flakes into reserved cooking liquid and simmer 2 minutes.

Add linguine, basil, remaining 12 clams in their shells, and any liquid in bowl and toss well with salt and pepper to taste.

Each serving about 300 calories and 5 grams fat

Photo opposite

PASTA "RAGS" WITH A THOUSAND HERBS

Serves 2 with leftovers

FOR SAUCE
½   cup fresh flat-leaf parsley, chopped
½   cup fresh basil, chopped
¼   cup chopped fresh tarragon
2   tablespoons chopped fresh mint
2   tablespoons chopped fresh thyme
1   tablespoon chopped fresh marjoram,
     or to taste
8   small fresh sage leaves, finely chopped
1½   teaspoons finely chopped fresh rosemary
½   cup extra-virgin olive oil

1   lb store-bought fresh pasta sheets*, cut with
     a ridged pastry wheel into 4- by 1-inch strips
½   cup freshly grated Pecorino Romano
2   medium vine-ripened tomatoes, peeled,
     seeded, and chopped

*available at specialty foods shops

MAKE SAUCE:
Stir together all sauce ingredients with salt and pepper to taste in a large bowl.

Cook pasta in a 6-quart pot of boiling salted water until al dente and drain. Add pasta to sauce and toss. Add cheese and toss again. Sprinkle pasta with tomatoes.

Photo on page 117

FUSILLI WITH ARUGULA AND SMOKED MOZZARELLA

Serves 2

- 4 oz dried *fusilli* or other spiral-shaped pasta
- 6 oz red and yellow grape or pear tomatoes, halved
- 2 tablespoons chopped red onion
- 2 tablespoons extra-virgin olive oil
- 1 tablespoon balsamic vinegar
- 1 bunch arugula, large stems removed and leaves cut into ¼-inch-wide strips
- ½ lb smoked mozzarella, cut into ¼-inch dice

Cook pasta in a large pot of boiling salted water until al dente.

While pasta is cooking, toss tomatoes and onion with oil and vinegar in a large bowl and season generously with salt and pepper.

Reserve ¼ cup pasta cooking water and drain pasta. Toss pasta, cooking water, arugula, and mozzarella with tomato mixture.

Serve immediately.

PASTA WITH CAPERS, GARLIC, AND BREAD CRUMBS

Serves 4

- ¾ lb *gigli di semola* or other short spiral pasta
- 4 garlic cloves, finely chopped
- ½ cup extra-virgin olive oil
- 6 tablespoons drained capers, finely chopped
- ¼ cup chopped fresh flat-leaf parsley
- ⅔ cup coarse dry bread crumbs
  Freshly grated parmesan (optional)

Cook pasta in a 6-quart pot of boiling salted water until al dente.

While pasta is cooking, cook garlic in oil in a large heavy skillet over moderate heat, stirring, just until pale golden, about 2 minutes. Stir in capers, parsley, and bread crumbs and cook, stirring, until bread crumbs and garlic are golden, 1 to 2 minutes.

Drain pasta and transfer to a heated large bowl. Pour sauce over pasta and toss to combine.

Serve pasta with parmesan.

Photo below

ORZO RISOTTO WITH BACON AND BUTTERNUT SQUASH

Serves 4

5   oz bacon (8 to 10 slices)
2   cups hot chicken broth
2   cups water
1   tablespoon olive oil
1   small butternut squash (1 lb), peeled, seeded, and cut into 1/2-inch dice
1   medium onion, chopped
1   teaspoon chopped fresh sage
1   cup *orzo* (rice-shaped pasta)
2   tablespoons chopped fresh flat-leaf parsley

Cook bacon in a heavy 3-quart saucepan until crisp. Drain on paper towels and crumble. Pour off all but 1 tablespoon drippings.

Bring broth and water to a simmer in a saucepan. Add oil to drippings and cook squash, onion, and sage over moderate heat, stirring frequently, until onion is softened. Stir in *orzo* and cook, stirring, 1 minute. Add hot broth and water mixture, 1/2 cup at a time, and cook at a high simmer, stirring constantly, until liquid is absorbed. Continue cooking, adding broth mixture, 1/2 cup at a time, until *orzo* is al dente, squash is tender, and mixture appears creamy, about 15 minutes. Season with salt and pepper.

Serve topped with bacon and parsley.

FETTUCCINE WITH PUMPKIN SEED PESTO

Serves 4 to 6

1   lb dried fettuccine or linguine
1   cup hulled green pumpkin seeds*
2   garlic cloves, minced
1/2 teaspoon cumin
1/4 teaspoon cayenne
3   tablespoons extra-virgin olive oil
2   tablespoons fresh lemon juice, or to taste
1/2 cup chopped fresh cilantro
2   scallions, chopped

available at natural foods stores

Cook pasta in a large pot of boiling salted water until al dente.

While pasta is boiling, cook pumpkin seeds, garlic, cumin, and cayenne in 2 tablespoons oil in a heavy skillet over moderate heat, stirring, until seeds plump and are toasted.

Reserve 1 1/2 cups pasta cooking water and drain pasta. Finely chop seed mixture in a food processor. Add remaining tablespoon oil and 1/2 cup cooking water and purée. Season with lemon juice and salt and pepper.

Transfer pesto to a large bowl and stir in cilantro. Toss pasta with pesto, adding enough remaining cooking water, 1/4 cup at a time, until sauce coats pasta but is slightly loose.

Sprinkle with scallions and serve immediately.

SPICY SOBA NOODLES WITH BROILED EGGPLANT

Serves 2

2   Asian eggplants (1 lb), cut lengthwise into ¼-inch-thick slices
5   tablespoons *mirin**
4   tablespoons soy sauce
2   tablespoons vegetable oil
5   oz *soba* noodles*
1   teaspoon chile paste with garlic, or to taste
¾   cup water
1   teaspoon cornstarch
1   tablespoon grated peeled fresh ginger
3   chopped scallions

    **available at natural foods stores and Asian markets*

Preheat broiler.

Arrange eggplant in 1 layer on a lightly oiled baking sheet. Stir together 2 tablespoons *mirin*, 1 tablespoon soy sauce, and 1 tablespoon oil and brush on eggplant. Broil until lightly browned and tender, 3 to 5 minutes. (Watch eggplant carefully as it can easily burn.) When cool enough to handle, cut diagonally into 1-inch-wide strips.

Cook noodles in a large pot of boiling water until al dente, about 6 minutes. Drain.

While *soba* are cooking, stir together remaining 3 tablespoons *mirin*, 3 tablespoons soy sauce, chile paste, water, and cornstarch.

Heat remaining tablespoon oil in a small saucepan until hot but not smoking. Add ginger and half of scallions and cook, stirring, until fragrant, 30 seconds. Add *mirin* mixture and bring to a boil, stirring. Simmer until slightly thickened, about 2 minutes, and season with salt.

Serve *soba* tossed with sauce and eggplant and topped with remaining scallions.

ASIAN SHRIMP AND NOODLES

Serves 4

Fresh wheat-flour Chinese noodles can usually be found in the produce section of your supermarket next to the tofu. If not, you can substitute 8 oz dried Chinese noodles; they take about the same amount of time to cook.

1   lb large shrimp, shelled and deveined
2   tablespoons vegetable oil
2   tablespoons finely chopped peeled fresh ginger
¼   cup chopped shallot
1   chopped jalapeño chile (half of seeds removed)
2½   cups chicken broth
½   cup water
2   tablespoons fresh lime juice
1   tablespoon sugar
1   tablespoon Asian fish sauce
12   oz fresh Chinese noodles (not rice noodles)
¼   cup chopped fresh mint
¼   cup chopped fresh cilantro

Accompaniments:
grated carrot, chopped scallion, and lime wedges

Season shrimp with salt. Heat 1 tablespoon oil in a 12-inch heavy skillet over moderately high heat until hot but not smoking. Add 1 tablespoon ginger, half of shallot, and half of jalapeño and stir-fry, stirring, 1 minute. Add shrimp and stir-fry just until cooked through, 2 to 3 minutes. Transfer to a bowl.

Heat remaining tablespoon oil in skillet over moderate heat until hot but not smoking and cook remaining tablespoon ginger, remaining shallot, and remaining jalapeño, stirring, until browned. Add broth and water and bring to a boil, stirring and scraping up any browned bits. Simmer 5 minutes, then stir in lime juice, sugar, and fish sauce.

Cook noodles in a large pot of boiling water until al dente, about 3 minutes. Drain and add to broth mixture with shrimp, mint, and cilantro. Cook over moderately low heat just until heated through.

GREEN NOODLES WITH GARLIC
Serves 2

½   lb dried spinach linguine
2   or 3 garlic cloves
3   tablespoons olive oil
⅓   cup freshly grated parmesan (1 oz)
½   cup fresh cilantro, chopped

Cook linguine in a pot of boiling salted water until al dente.

While pasta is cooking, force garlic cloves through a garlic press into a 10- to 12-inch skillet and add oil. Cook garlic over moderately low heat, stirring, until fragrant, 1 to 2 minutes.

Ladle out and reserve about ¼ cup pasta cooking water. Drain linguine and add to garlic mixture. Cook over moderate heat, tossing pasta until coated well, about 1 minute. (If pasta appears dry, add reserved pasta cooking water, 1 tablespoon at a time.) Add parmesan and toss linguine until cheese begins to melt. Remove from heat and toss linguine with cilantro and salt and pepper to taste.

TORTELLINI WITH BABY SPINACH AND GARLIC
Serves 4

1   (15- to 16-oz) package frozen cheese tortellini
2   tablespoons extra-virgin olive oil
2   garlic cloves, minced
8   cups baby spinach (8 oz), tough stems removed
¼   cup parmesan shavings

Cook pasta in a large pot of boiling salted water until al dente. Reserve ¼ cup cooking water and drain pasta.

While pasta is cooking, heat olive oil in a 12-inch nonstick skillet over moderate heat until hot but not smoking. Cook garlic, stirring, until fragrant, about 30 seconds. Add spinach and cook, stirring, until just wilted, 2 to 3 minutes.

Toss pasta with spinach and cooking water and season with salt and pepper.

Sprinkle with parmesan and serve immediately.

MALFADA WITH SMOKED SALMON AND SUGAR SNAP PEAS

Serves 2

½ lb sugar snap peas, trimmed
4 oz dried *malfada* or fettuccine
1 shallot, chopped
1 tablespoon unsalted butter
½ cup heavy cream
2 tablespoons chopped fresh dill
1 tablespoon coarse-grained mustard
1 teaspoon fresh lemon juice
4 oz smoked salmon, cut into ½-inch-wide strips

Bring a large pot of salted water to a boil. Have ready a bowl of ice and water. Cook peas in boiling water until bright green, 1 minute. Transfer to ice water with a slotted spoon. Cook pasta in boiling water until al dente.

While pasta is cooking, drain sugar snap peas and cut diagonally into 1-inch pieces. Cook shallot in butter in a large nonstick skillet over moderate heat until softened. Add cream, dill, and mustard and heat, stirring, until hot. Stir in lemon juice and salt and pepper to taste.

Reserve ¼ cup pasta cooking water and drain pasta. Toss together pasta, cooking water, salmon, peas, and cream mixture in a large bowl.

Serve immediately.

GEMELLI WITH OLIVADA AND ROASTED RED PEPPERS

Serves 2

6 oz *gemelli* or penne
2 tablespoons bottled *olivada* or black-olive paste
1 drained bottled roasted red pepper, cut into 1-inch pieces
2 tablespoons chopped fresh flat-leaf parsley
¼ cup crumbled feta

Cook pasta in a large pot of boiling salted water until al dente. Reserve ¼ cup cooking water and drain pasta.

Toss pasta with *olivada*, roasted red pepper, and parsley, adding pasta cooking water 2 tablespoons at a time, until sauce coats pasta but is slightly loose and season with salt and pepper.

Sprinkle with feta and serve immediately.

CAMPANELLE WITH LEMON TOMATILLO SAUCE

Serves 4

1 lb tomatillos, husked
2 garlic cloves
2 tablespoons olive oil
½ teaspoon ground cumin
½ teaspoon freshly grated lemon zest
½ cup heavy cream
12 oz dried *campanelle* or rotini pasta

ACCOMPANIMENTS:
coarsely chopped fresh cilantro and crumbled *cotija* cheese or freshly grated parmesan

Heat a cast-iron skillet over moderate heat until hot. Roast tomatillos and garlic, turning with tongs, until blackened in spots (garlic will blacken first), about 10 minutes. Pulse tomatillos and garlic to a coarse purée in a food processor.

Heat oil in a large skillet over moderate heat until hot but not smoking, then cook cumin, stirring, until fragrant, about 30 seconds. Stir in zest and tomatillo purée and simmer, stirring frequently, 5 minutes. Add cream and simmer 5 minutes. Season with salt and pepper.

Cook pasta in a large pot of boiling salted water until al dente. Reserve ½ cup pasta cooking water and drain pasta. Toss pasta with tomatillo sauce, adding pasta cooking water ¼ cup at a time, until sauce coats pasta but is slightly loose. Serve immediately.

PASTA FAGIOLE
Serves 4

2 tablespoons extra-virgin olive oil
1 garlic clove, minced
4 cups chicken broth
1 (14-oz) can stewed tomatoes with Italian seasoning
1 (19-oz) can *cannellini* beans, rinsed
6 oz *tubetti* or *ditalini* pasta
3 tablespoons chopped fresh basil
2 tablespoons freshly grated parmesan

ACCOMPANIMENT:
grilled or toasted Italian bread

Heat 1 tablespoon oil in a 3-quart saucepan over moderate heat until hot but not smoking, then cook garlic, stirring, until fragrant, about 30 seconds. Stir in broth and tomatoes with their juices and bring to a boil, breaking up tomatoes with a fork.

Add beans, pasta, 2 tablespoons basil, and parmesan and boil, stirring frequently, until pasta is al dente. Let stand 5 minutes. (Pasta will continue to absorb liquid.) Stir in remaining tablespoon basil and pepper to taste.

Drizzle with remaining tablespoon oil and serve immediately.

COOKING PASTA

When it comes to cooking their pasta, *Gourmet*'s food editors have particular guidelines:

· Start out by bringing a large pot of cold water (5 to 6 quarts of water for a pound of pasta) to a rapid boil.

· Once the water boils, add plenty of salt (about 2 ½ to 3 heaping tablespoons) and allow the water to return to a rapid boil.

· Add the pasta all at once (to assure even cooking), without breaking long pasta strands in half (instead, bend it with a wooden spoon, forcing the strands under the water). Immediately stir the pasta well to avoid sticking, and cover the pot until the water returns to a boil. Then, uncover the pot and cook at a rapid boil, stirring once or twice during the cooking, until the pasta is al dente. *Do not add oil to the water or the pasta won't stick to the sauce!* Al dente means "firm to the bite" (just tender, yet with still some resistance to the tooth). Reserve a little cooking water before you drain the pasta, in case you want to thin the sauce.

· Drain the pasta in a colander (never rinse pasta, except for cold pasta dishes), giving the colander a few vigorous shakes, and immediately toss with sauce. Serve at once.

—Diane Keitt

PASTA WITH MUSSELS, ROASTED RED PEPPERS, AND BROCCOLI RABE

Serves 2 generously

Mustard greens or broccoli may be substituted for the broccoli rabe.

4   oz broccoli rabe (coarse stems discarded), cut into 2-inch pieces
⅓   lb *caserrecci* or other short pasta such as penne or *gemelli*
3   tablespoons extra-virgin olive oil
3   garlic cloves, minced
1   lb mussels, cleaned and beards removed
⅓   cup dry white wine
¼   teaspoon dried hot red pepper flakes
2   red bell peppers, roasted (procedure follows) and cut into 1-inch-thick strips
1   tablespoon balsamic vinegar
2   tablespoons chopped fresh flat-leaf parsley

Preheat broiler.

Have ready a bowl of ice and cold water. Cook broccoli rabe in boiling water 5 minutes, or until just tender, and with a slotted spoon transfer to ice water to stop cooking. Drain and pat dry. Transfer to a bowl.

Cook pasta in same boiling water until al dente and drain.

While pasta is cooking, heat oil in a large heavy skillet over moderate heat until hot but not smoking, then cook garlic, stirring, until softened, about 1 minute. Add mussels and toss to coat. Add wine and red pepper flakes and cook, covered, over moderately high heat 3 minutes, or until mussels begin to open. Add broccoli rabe, roasted peppers, and salt and pepper to taste and toss until heated through. (Discard any unopened mussels.)

Add pasta to skillet, tossing well, and transfer to a deep platter or shallow bowl. Drizzle vinegar over pasta and sprinkle with parsley.

Photo opposite

TO QUICK ROAST AND PEEL PEPPERS

BROILER METHOD:
Preheat broiler.

Quarter peppers lengthwise, discarding stems, seeds, and ribs. Put peppers, skin sides up, on rack of broiler pan and broil about 2 inches from heat until skins are blistered and charred, 8 to 12 minutes.

GAS STOVE METHOD:
Lay whole peppers on their sides on racks of burners (preferably 1 to a burner) and turn flames on high. Char peppers, turning them with tongs, until skins are blackened, 5 to 8 minutes.

Transfer peppers roasted by either method to a bowl and let stand, covered with plastic wrap, until cool enough to handle. Peel peppers and if necessary cut off tops and discard seeds and ribs.

COUSCOUS AND SUGAR SNAP PEA SALAD WITH PISTACHIOS

Serves 2

1   cup water
½   teaspoon salt
1   cup sugar snap peas, trimmed and cut diagonally into ½-inch pieces
½   cup couscous
1   large carrot, peeled and coarsely grated
2   tablespoons chopped pistachios, toasted
2   tablespoons chopped fresh mint
       FOR DRESSING
2   tablespoons fresh orange juice
2   teaspoons honey
1   teaspoon fresh lemon juice
1   teaspoon extra-virgin olive oil
¼   teaspoon cumin
¼   teaspoon cayenne

Have ready a bowl of ice and cold water. Bring 1 cup water to a boil with salt in a small saucepan and cook peas until bright green, about 1 minute. Remove peas with a slotted spoon and refresh in ice water. Drain well.

Return water in saucepan to a boil and add couscous. Remove from heat and cover. Let stand 5 minutes and fluff with a fork. Let stand, covered, 3 minutes more. Transfer to a bowl and add peas, carrot, pistachios, and mint.

MAKE DRESSING:
Whisk together all dressing ingredients.

Toss together couscous, dressing, and salt and pepper to taste.

Each serving about 362 calories and 10 grams fat

ORECCHIETTE WITH TURKEY SAUSAGE AND MARINARA SAUCE

Serves 6

If you can't get Italian turkey sausage in casings at your supermarket, you can substitute regular or breakfast turkey sausage mixed with ¼ teaspoon dried hot red pepper flakes.

2   teaspoons olive oil
1   medium onion, cut into ¼-inch wedges
2   links hot Italian turkey sausage (4 oz), casings removed
½   cup dry white wine
1   cup bottled fat-free or low-fat marinara sauce
½   cup water
1   lb *orecchiette* or small shell pasta
2   tablespoons chopped fresh flat-leaf parsley

Heat oil in a large nonstick skillet over moderate heat until hot but not smoking. Cook onion, stirring occasionally, until softened. Crumble turkey sausage into skillet and cook, breaking up clumps with a fork, just until no longer pink. Add wine and simmer until reduced by half. Stir in marinara sauce and water and simmer until slightly thickened, about 10 minutes.

While sauce is simmering, cook pasta in a large pot of boiling salted water until al dente.

Reserve ½ cup cooking water and drain pasta.

Add parsley to sauce and season with salt and pepper. Toss pasta with sauce, adding cooking water 2 tablespoons at a time, until sauce coats pasta but is slightly loose. Serve immediately.

Each serving about 288 calories and 6 grams fat

SPAGHETTI WITH RAMPS

Serves 4

½ lb ramps
1 teaspoon finely grated fresh lemon zest
¼ cup extra-virgin olive oil
1 lb spaghetti
2 tablespoons freshly grated parmesan

ACCOMPANIMENT:
toasted bread-crumb topping (recipe follows)

Trim roots from ramps and slip off outer skin on bulbs if loose. Blanch ramps in a 6-quart pot of boiling salted water, 2 to 3 seconds, and transfer to a cutting board with tongs. Coarsely chop ramps and put in a blender with zest and oil.

Add spaghetti to boiling water and cook a few minutes, then ladle out ½ cup pasta water and add to blender. Purée ramps until smooth and season with salt.

Continue to cook spaghetti until al dente, then ladle out about 1 cup additional pasta water before draining spaghetti in a colander. Return pasta to pot with ramp purée and toss with parmesan over moderate heat 1 to 2 minutes, thinning sauce with a little pasta water as needed to coat pasta.

Photo right

TOASTED BREAD-CRUMB TOPPING FOR PASTA

Makes about 1½ cups

3 (½-inch-thick) slices whole-grain bread
2 tablespoons extra-virgin olive oil
  Sea salt to taste

Preheat oven to 350°F.

Cut bread into cubes, then grind to crumbs in a food processor. Spread in a shallow baking pan and bake in middle of oven, stirring occasionally, until golden, 10 to 15 minutes. Pour crumbs into a bowl and stir in oil and salt.

GRILLED SMOKED-MOZZARELLA AND YELLOW SQUASH PIZZETTES

Serves 2

You'll need to purchase a 1-lb package of frozen pizza dough, even though only a quarter of that is called for here. Refreeze the remainder for another use.

1   teaspoon extra-virgin olive oil
1   yellow squash (½ lb), thinly sliced
1   plum tomato, halved and thinly sliced lengthwise
2   tablespoons shredded fresh basil
¼   lb frozen pizza dough, thawed
    Cornmeal for dusting baking sheet
2   tablespoons coarsely grated smoked mozzarella

Prepare grill.

Heat oil in a large nonstick skillet over moderate heat until hot but not smoking, then cook squash with salt and pepper to taste, stirring frequently, 2 minutes. Add tomato and cook until squash is barely tender, 2 to 3 minutes. Remove from heat and stir in basil.

Divide dough into 4 pieces. Rotate and stretch each piece into a 4-inch round on a floured surface with floured hands. (Do not roll out, as dough has too much elasticity and will shrink.) Put rounds in one layer on cornmeal-dusted baking sheet.

Grill rounds, cornmeal sides up, on a lightly oiled rack set 5 to 6 inches over glowing coals until undersides are golden, 2 to 3 minutes. If crusts puff up in the center, prick with a fork to allow air to escape. Flip crusts over with a metal spatula and top each with one fourth squash mixture. Sprinkle pizzettes with mozzarella and grill until undersides are golden and cheese is melted, about 2 minutes.

Each serving (2 pizzettes) about 206 calories and 4 grams fat

Photo below

PESTO EGGPLANT PIZZA

Serves 4

Cornmeal for sprinkling
½ large eggplant, halved lengthwise
and cut crosswise into ⅛-inch-thick slices
3 tablespoons extra-virgin olive oil
1 cup fresh basil
2 garlic cloves, smashed
4 tablespoons freshly grated parmesan
2 tablespoons pine nuts
1 lb fresh or thawed frozen pizza dough
All-purpose flour for dusting
3 plum tomatoes, cored and coarsely chopped

Arrange oven racks on lowest and middle shelves and preheat oven to 500°F. Lightly oil a 17- by 14-inch heavy baking sheet (without sides) and sprinkle with cornmeal, tapping off excess.

Arrange eggplant in 1 layer on an oiled shallow baking pan and brush with 2 tablespoons oil. Bake eggplant in middle of oven until tender and beginning to brown, about 5 minutes. Cool.

Purée basil, garlic, 2 tablespoons parmesan, pine nuts, and remaining tablespoon oil in a food processor and season with salt and pepper.

Dust dough and your hands with flour. Holding 1 edge of dough in the air with both hands and letting bottom touch work surface, move hands around edge (like turning a steering wheel), letting weight of dough stretch itself into roughly a 10-inch round. Flour backs of fists and with them stretch dough from center of underside, turning dough to maintain a rough circle, until about 13 to 14 inches in diameter. Put on baking sheet.

Scatter eggplant over dough, leaving a 1-inch border around edge, and dot with pesto. Sprinkle with tomatoes, remaining 2 tablespoons parmesan, and salt and pepper to taste.

Bake pizza in bottom of oven until dough is browned and crisp and topping is bubbling, 12 to 15 minutes.

Cut into wedges and serve.

PIZZA MARGHERITA

Serves 4

Cornmeal for sprinkling
1 lb fresh or thawed frozen pizza dough
All-purpose flour for dusting
⅓ lb fresh mozzarella, coarsely grated
4 ripe plum tomatoes, cored and thinly sliced lengthwise
1 tablespoon minced garlic
½ teaspoon dried oregano, crumbled
2 tablespoons extra-virgin olive oil

Arrange oven rack on lowest shelf and preheat oven to 500°F. Lightly oil a 17- by 14-inch heavy baking sheet (without sides) and sprinkle with cornmeal, tapping off excess.

Dust dough and your hands with flour. Holding 1 edge of dough in the air with both hands and letting bottom touch work surface, move hands around edge (like turning a steering wheel), letting weight of dough stretch itself into roughly a 10-inch round. Flour backs of fists and with them stretch dough from center of underside, turning dough to maintain a rough circle, until about 13 to 14 inches in diameter. Put on baking sheet.

Sprinkle mozzarella over dough, leaving 1-inch border around edge, and arrange tomato slices on cheese. Cook garlic and oregano in oil over low heat until garlic is fragrant, about 1 minute, and spoon over tomatoes.

Bake pizza in bottom of oven until dough is browned and crisp and topping is bubbling, 12 to 15 minutes, and season with salt and pepper.

Cut into wedges and serve.

WHITE BEAN, TOMATO, AND GOAT CHEESE PIZZA

Serves 4

Cornmeal for sprinkling

1 cup canned *cannellini* beans, rinsed

1 garlic clove, smashed

1 tablespoon fat-free chicken broth or water

1½ teaspoons extra-virgin olive oil

1 lb fresh or thawed frozen pizza dough
All-purpose flour for dusting

3 plum tomatoes, cored and coarsely chopped

¼ small red onion, thinly sliced

1 teaspoon chopped fresh rosemary

4 oz low-fat soft goat cheese, crumbled

2 cups baby greens, such as arugula or *mâche*

Arrange oven rack on lowest shelf and preheat oven to 500°F. Lightly oil a 17- by 14-inch heavy baking sheet (without sides) and sprinkle with cornmeal, tapping off excess.

Pulse beans, garlic, broth, and 1 teaspoon oil in a food processor until coarsely chopped and season with salt and pepper.

Dust dough and your hands with flour. Holding 1 edge of dough in the air with both hands and letting bottom touch work surface, move hands around edge (like turning a steering wheel), letting weight of dough stretch itself into roughly a 10-inch round. Flour backs of fists and with them stretch dough from center of underside, turning dough to maintain a rough circle, until about 13 to 14 inches in diameter. Put on baking sheet.

Spread bean purée over dough, leaving a 1-inch border around edge. Top purée with tomatoes and onion, then sprinkle with rosemary and dot with cheese. Season with salt and pepper.

Bake pizza in bottom of oven until dough is browned and crisp and topping is bubbling, 12 to 15 minutes.

Toss baby greens with remaining ½ teaspoon oil and salt and pepper to taste and sprinkle over pizza.

Cut into wedges and serve.

Each serving (2 slices) 691 calories and 9 grams fat

BROCCOLI RABE PIZZA

Serves 4

    Cornmeal for sprinkling
2   tablespoons extra-virgin olive oil
1   tablespoon minced garlic
¼   teaspoon dried hot red pepper flakes
1   bunch broccoli rabe, tough stems discarded
    and leaves and florets cut into 2-inch pieces
⅔   cup water
1   lb fresh or thawed frozen pizza dough
    All-purpose flour for dusting
1½   oz shaved parmesan

Arrange oven rack on lowest shelf and preheat oven to 500°F. Lightly oil a 17- by 14-inch heavy baking sheet (without sides) and sprinkle with cornmeal, tapping off excess.

Heat oil in a 12-inch heavy skillet over moderate heat until hot but not smoking, then cook garlic and red pepper flakes, stirring, until fragrant, about 30 seconds. Add broccoli rabe and cook, stirring, until wilted, 3 to 4 minutes. Add water and simmer until water has evaporated and broccoli rabe is just tender, about 5 minutes. Cool and season with salt and pepper.

Dust dough and your hands with flour. Holding 1 edge of dough in the air with both hands and letting bottom touch work surface, move hands around edge (like turning a steering wheel), letting weight of dough stretch itself into roughly a 10-inch round. Flour backs of fists and with them stretch dough from center of underside, turning dough to maintain a rough circle, until about 13 to 14 inches in diameter. Put on baking sheet.

Scatter broccoli rabe mixture over dough, leaving a 1-inch border around edge.

Bake pizza in bottom of oven until dough is browned and crisp, 12 to 15 minutes. Sprinkle cheese over pizza and bake until cheese starts to melt, 1 minute more.

Cut into wedges and serve.

RED AND YELLOW BELL PEPPER CALZONES

Serves 4

    Cornmeal for sprinkling
1   large red bell pepper, cut into ¼-inch strips
1   large yellow bell pepper, cut into ¼-inch strips
1   large onion, cut into ¼-inch strips
1   teaspoon chopped fresh rosemary
1½   tablespoons extra-virgin olive oil
2   oz sliced prosciutto, cut crosswise into
    ¼-inch strips (optional)
5   oz Danish Fontina, cut into ½-inch cubes
1   lb fresh or thawed frozen pizza dough
    All-purpose flour for dusting

Arrange oven rack on lowest shelf and preheat oven to 500°F. Lightly oil a 17- by 14-inch heavy baking sheet without sides and sprinkle with cornmeal, tapping off excess.

Cook bell peppers, onion, and rosemary in oil in a large heavy skillet over moderate heat until vegetables are softened, 10 to 12 minutes. Stir in prosciutto and salt and pepper to taste. Cool and stir in cheese.

Quarter dough and form each quarter into a disk. Dust dough and your hands with flour. Working with 1 quarter at a time, holding 1 edge of dough in the air with both hands and letting bottom touch work surface, move hands around edge (like turning a steering wheel), letting weight of dough stretch itself into roughly an 8-inch round.

Spread one fourth of filling on half of 1 circle and fold dough over to form a half moon, pinching edges to seal. Starting at one corner, fold and roll dough over to form a decorative edge. Transfer to baking sheet and make more calzones in same manner.

Bake calzones in bottom of oven until dough is puffed, browned, and crisp, 12 to 15 minutes. Cool 5 minutes before serving.

QUICK VEGETABLES

Designed to complement our stove-top dishes and grills, here are a host of familiar vegetable favorites prepared in simple yet unfamiliar ways. Corn is grilled on the cob and served Mexican-style with crumbled cheese and lime. Tomatoes are sliced and drizzled with a vibrant *salsa verde*. Sweet potato wedges are roasted with soy sauce and toasted sesame seeds. Even everyday carrots get an exotic Moroccan kick with cumin and coriander. Try one recipe or make a few all at once for a knock-out vegetable feast.

CORN ON THE COB WITH CHEESE AND LIME

Serves 2

These messy but irresistible ears of corn coated with cheese are a popular street snack in Mexico. For our recipe we used cotija, a crumbly, pungent, aged-curd cheese that can range in consistency from soft to very hard, depending on the brand. (We made ours with Los Fortales, a hard variety available at cheese shops and some specialty foods shops.) You can, however, substitute feta, which is more widely available.

4   ears of corn in the husk
1/4 cup mayonnaise
1/8 teaspoon cayenne, or to taste
4   oz *cotija* or feta

ACCOMPANIMENT:
lime wedges

Prepare grill.

Soak corn in husks in cold water 10 minutes. Drain corn and grill on a rack set 5 to 6 inches over glowing coals until husks are charred, about 10 minutes. Shuck corn and grill until kernels are browned in spots, about 10 minutes.

While corn is grilling, whisk together mayonnaise and cayenne. Grate *cotija* or feta using the small teardrop-shaped holes on a four-sided grater.

Brush mayonnaise mixture onto hot corn and sprinkle with *cotija.* Recipe may be doubled to serve 4.

Photo opposite

BROILED LEEKS WITH BUTTERED BREAD CRUMBS

Serves 2

3   medium leeks (1 1/2 lb), trimmed and most of dark-green parts discarded
2   tablespoons unsalted butter
3   tablespoons fine dry bread crumbs

Cut leeks in half lengthwise and wash well (keep halves intact). Steam 15 minutes, or until tender. Arrange leeks, cut sides up, on a buttered baking sheet.

Preheat broiler.

Melt butter and stir in bread crumbs and salt and pepper to taste. Spoon bread-crumb mixture onto leeks, patting down mixture with back of spoon to help adhere. Broil 2 to 3 inches from heat until bread crumbs are golden brown, about 3 minutes. Recipe may be doubled to serve 4.

Photo on page 135

SESAME-SOY SWEET POTATOES
Serves 4 to 6

1½ lb sweet potatoes, halved crosswise
    and each half cut into 8 wedges
2   tablespoons olive oil
1   tablespoon sesame seeds, toasted
3   tablespoons soy sauce

Preheat oven to 450°F.

Toss potatoes with oil in a shallow baking pan. Roast in middle of oven until almost tender, about 15 minutes. Toss with sesame seeds and roast until potatoes are tender, about 3 minutes more. Drizzle soy sauce over potatoes and roast until almost evaporated, 1 to 2 minutes. Season with salt and pepper.

SUCCOTASH
Serves 8

¼   lb sliced bacon
1   small onion, chopped
2   garlic cloves, minced
    Kernels from 4 ears corn
1   large fresh jalapeño chile, seeded
    and finely chopped
1   (10-oz) box frozen baby lima beans, thawed
½   lb fresh okra, cut into ⅓-inch-thick slices
¾   lb cherry tomatoes, halved
2   tablespoons cider vinegar, or to taste
¼   cup chopped fresh basil

Cook bacon in a large skillet over moderate heat until crisp. Drain on paper towels, reserving fat in skillet, and crumble. Cook onion in fat in skillet over moderate heat until softened. Add garlic and cook, stirring, 1 minute. Stir in corn, jalapeño, lima beans, okra, and tomatoes and cook, stirring, until vegetables are tender, about 7 minutes. Stir in vinegar, basil, and salt and pepper to taste.

Serve succotash topped with crumbled bacon.

HERBED POTATO SALAD
Serves 6

Some varieties of fresh thyme are stronger than others, so we've given a range. Try starting with 2 teaspoons and adding a third if you need more flavor. And, whatever you do, don't stint on the salt!

2   lb boiling potatoes
¼   cup fresh flat-leaf parsley, chopped
2   to 3 teaspoons fresh thyme, chopped
3   tablespoons olive oil (preferably
    extra-virgin)
1   tablespoon minced shallot

Cover potatoes with cold salted water by 2 inches in a 5-quart pot and simmer until just tender when tested with a wooden skewer, 10 minutes (for small fingerling potatoes) to 25 minutes (for larger boiling or all-purpose potatoes). Drain and cool to room temperature.

Cut potatoes into 1½-inch pieces. Gently toss potatoes in a bowl with herbs, oil, shallot, and salt and pepper to taste. Serve at room temperature.

Photo opposite, top

MOROCCAN SPICY CARROTS

Serves 4

Because a food processor grates the carrots too fine, we recommend that you grate them by hand for this recipe. Be sure to use the side of a grater with teardrop-shaped holes instead of the kind that look like the metal has been punched out from the back. The punched-out kind will turn the carrots to mush.

2	tablespoons golden raisins
1/8	teaspoon crumbled saffron threads
1	tablespoon plus 1 teaspoon hot water
4	large carrots, cut into 3-inch lengths
2	teaspoons ground coriander seeds
1/2	teaspoon ground cumin
1	tablespoon olive or vegetable oil
1	tablespoon finely chopped fresh cilantro

Stir together raisins, saffron, and water and let stand 30 minutes to soften raisins.

While raisin mixture is standing, grate sides of carrots using side of a grater with teardrop-shaped holes, discarding woody center cores. Stir together coriander seeds, cumin, and oil in a small heavy skillet and cook over moderate heat until fragrant, about 1 minute.

Toss together carrots, raisin mixture, spices, and cilantro in a bowl and season with salt and pepper.

Photo left, bottom

PEELING

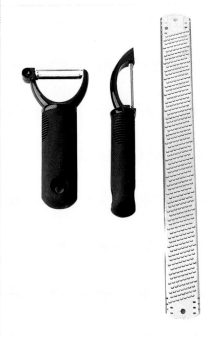

We think every kitchen needs a **Y-peeler** (above, left) as well as a regulation **swivel peeler** (above, middle). Once you've tried the former out on round foods such as butternut squash or a pie's worth of apples, you'll understand why. A rasplike **zester** by Microplane (above, right) will give you the fluffiest, most amazing lemon zest you've ever seen, with no damage to knuckles or manicure. (It's good for nutmeg and parmesan, too.)

—Zanne Stewart

BROCCOLI RABE
Serves 2

½ bunch broccoli rabe (5 oz), hollow stems trimmed

Cook broccoli rabe in boiling salted water until just tender, about 4 minutes. Drain and season with salt and pepper.

Each serving about 20 calories and less than 1 gram fat

Photo on page 62

CRISP POTATO GALETTES
Serves 2

Olive-oil cooking spray
1 (8-oz) russet (baking) potato

Preheat oven to 400°F. Lightly coat a large baking sheet with cooking spray.

Peel potato and cut crosswise into paper-thin slices with a *mandoline* or other manual slicer. Overlap 8 to 10 slices on baking sheet to form a 4-inch round and make 7 more rounds in the same manner. Spray rounds lightly with cooking spray and season with salt and pepper.

Bake until golden brown and crisp, 15 to 20 minutes, and season with salt.

Each serving about 88 calories and less than 1 gram fat

Photo on page 62

PICKLED CUCUMBER AND CABBAGE

Serves 2

⅓ English cucumber, halved lengthwise and thinly sliced crosswise
¼ small red cabbage, very thinly sliced
½ red onion, thinly sliced
½ cup rice vinegar (not seasoned)
⅓ cup sugar
¼ cup water
2 teaspoons salt

Combine cucumber, cabbage, and onion in a bowl. Bring remaining ingredients to a boil in saucepan, stirring, and immediately pour over cucumber mixture. Toss and let stand at room temperature, stirring occasionally, 10 minutes. If you prefer to serve cold, chill in freezer 15 minutes. Recipe may be doubled to serve 4.

Photo on page 59

CHIVE ZUCCHINI RIBBONS

Serves 4

2 lb small zucchini
½ cup chopped fresh chives
½ teaspoon fresh lemon zest
½ teaspoon fresh lime zest
2 teaspoons fresh lemon juice
1 tablespoon extra-virgin olive oil

Shave as many long ribbons as possible from zucchini with a U-shaped vegetable peeler. Stir together remaining ingredients in a large bowl.

Steam zucchini in a steamer set over boiling water, covered, turning with tongs halfway through steaming, until crisp-tender, about 2 minutes total. Transfer zucchini to chive mixture and gently toss. Season with salt and pepper.

Each serving about 64 calories and 3 grams fat

CURRIED PEAS WITH CILANTRO

Serves 6

3 tablespoons unsalted butter
2 shallots, finely chopped
1 teaspoon curry powder
½ teaspoon ground cumin
⅓ cup water
2 (10-oz) boxes frozen peas
½ cup chopped fresh cilantro

Heat butter in a large saucepan over moderate heat until foam subsides, then cook shallot until softened. Stir in curry powder, cumin, water, and peas and simmer until peas are just tender, about 5 minutes. Stir in cilantro and salt and pepper to taste.

TOMATOES WITH SALSA VERDE

Serves 6

FOR SALSA VERDE
1 cup fresh flat-leaf parsley
½ cup fresh basil
2 large garlic cloves
¼ cup water
2 tablespoons extra-virgin olive oil
1 tablespoon red-wine vinegar
1 tablespoon capers, rinsed
1 teaspoon anchovy paste

9 medium tomatoes, sliced

MAKE SALSA VERDE:
Blend all *salsa verde* ingredients in a blender until smooth and season with salt and pepper.

Arrange tomatoes on a platter and spoon sauce over them.

Each serving about 89 calories and 5 grams fat

CAULIFLOWER GOAT CHEESE GRATIN

Serves 4 to 6

2½ lb cauliflower, cut into florets
3   tablespoons unsalted butter
1   cup fresh bread crumbs
2   tablespoons finely chopped shallot
1   teaspoon all-purpose flour
1   cup half-and-half
4   oz soft mild goat cheese, crumbled

Preheat oven to 425°F.

Boil cauliflower in a large saucepan of boiling salted water until crisp-tender, about 7 minutes. Drain well and transfer to a 1½-quart casserole.

While cauliflower is boiling, heat 2 tablespoons butter in a 10-inch skillet over moderate heat until foam subsides, then toast bread crumbs with salt and pepper to taste, stirring, until golden brown, about 5 minutes. Transfer crumbs to a plate to cool.

Heat remaining tablespoon butter in a small saucepan over moderate heat until foam subsides, then cook shallot, stirring, until softened. Add flour and cook, stirring constantly, 1 minute. Whisk in half-and-half and goat cheese and simmer, whisking constantly, until cheese is melted and sauce is slightly thickened, about 3 minutes.

Pour sauce over cauliflower and top with toasted bread crumbs. Bake gratin in middle of oven until golden brown and sauce is bubbling, about 10 minutes.

ASPARAGUS WITH PEPERONATA

Serves 6

3   lb asparagus, trimmed
1   tablespoon olive oil
¼   cup finely chopped shallot
2   garlic cloves, minced
2   red bell peppers, finely chopped
1   tomato, seeded and chopped
¼   teaspoon dried hot red pepper flakes
2   tablespoons balsamic vinegar

Cook asparagus in a large saucepan of boiling salted water until crisp-tender, about 6 minutes. Drain and transfer to a bowl of ice and cold water to stop cooking. Drain asparagus well.

Heat oil in a large nonstick skillet over moderate heat until hot but not smoking, then cook shallot until just tender. Add garlic and cook, stirring, 1 minute. Stir in bell peppers, tomato, and red pepper flakes and cook over moderately high heat, stirring occasionally, until bell pepper is softened, about 5 minutes. Stir in vinegar and cook, stirring, until liquid is evaporated, about 2 minutes. Transfer *peperonata* to a bowl and chill, stirring occasionally, until slightly cooled, about 10 minutes.

Serve asparagus topped with *peperonata*.

Each serving about 65 calories and 2 grams fat

MASHED TURNIPS

Serves 4 to 6

- 2 lb turnips, peeled and cut into 1-inch pieces
- ½ lb boiling potatoes, peeled and cut into 1-inch pieces
- 2 tablespoons unsalted butter
- 1 tablespoon heavy cream
- ¼ teaspoon freshly grated nutmeg

Boil turnips and potatoes in salted water to cover in a large saucepan until tender, about 7 minutes. Drain well and transfer to a large bowl. Add butter, cream, and nutmeg and coarsely mash with a potato masher. Season with salt and pepper.

MASHED POTATOES

Serves 6

- 2½ lb Yukon Gold potatoes (about 5 large), peeled and quartered
- ¼ cup nonfat sour cream
  Pinch of freshly grated nutmeg

Cover potatoes with salted water and boil until tender, about 20 minutes. Drain in a colander set over a bowl, reserving cooking liquid, and return potatoes to pot. Mash potatoes with 1¼ cups cooking liquid and sour cream. Season with nutmeg and salt and pepper.

Each serving about 125 calories and less than 1 gram fat

mashing

The question of how best to mash potatoes has always been the subject of heated debate among the food editors. If you like your mash to be smooth, you may be tempted to try the procedure in the food processor. *Don't.* It will transform potatoes into the worst kind of glue! Three of our favorite implements for the job are shown here. The **food mill** (above, left) and the **ricer** (above, top) both guarantee lump-free spuds. The squiggly potato **masher** (above, right), like the cylindrical wooden club–type found in antiques shops, will give you a coarser, more textured mash.

—Zanne Stewart

POTATO SALAD WITH ASIAN-STYLE CHILE DRESSING

Serves 6

2   lb boiling potatoes (preferably yellow-fleshed), quartered lengthwise and cut crosswise into ¾-inch pieces
1   fresh jalapeño chile, minced with some seeds (wear rubber gloves)
2   small garlic cloves, minced
1   tablespoon sugar
1   tablespoon white-wine vinegar
1½ tablespoons fresh lime juice
1   tablespoon anchovy paste
1½ teaspoons vegetable oil
¼   cup fresh cilantro, finely chopped
¼   cup fresh mint, finely chopped
2   celery ribs, thinly sliced crosswise

Steam potatoes in a steamer set over boiling water, covered, 10 to 12 minutes, or until just tender. Transfer to a bowl and let cool to room temperature. Whisk together jalapeño, garlic, sugar, vinegar, lime juice, anchovy paste, oil, and salt to taste and let stand at room temperature 30 minutes. Add dressing to potatoes with cilantro, mint, and celery and toss.

Photo below

GREEN BEANS WITH PECAN PESTO

Serves 6 to 8

Left-over pesto will keep for 1 week, chilled. To avoid discoloration, be sure to cover the surface with plastic wrap.

FOR PECAN PESTO
½   cup pecans, toasted and chopped
½   cup fresh flat-leaf parsley
½   cup fresh cilantro
1   large garlic clove, chopped
½   cup extra-virgin olive oil

4   lb thin green beans or *haricots verts*, trimmed

MAKE PESTO:
Blend all pesto ingredients with salt and pepper to taste in a blender until almost smooth.

Cook beans in boiling salted water until crisp-tender, 3 to 5 minutes. Transfer to a bowl of ice and cold water to stop cooking and drain well. Toss beans with half of pesto, or to taste.

BABY CARROTS AND HARICOTS VERTS WITH MUSTARD-DILL SAUCE

Serves 6

1½ lb baby carrots, trimmed
½   lb *haricots verts* or thin green beans, trimmed
2½ tablespoons white-wine vinegar
¼   cup coarse-grained mustard
1   tablespoon Dijon mustard
1½ teaspoons light brown sugar
½   cup vegetable oil
1½ tablespoons chopped fresh dill

Cook carrots in a large saucepan of boiling salted water until tender, about 4 minutes. Transfer with a slotted spoon to a large bowl of ice and cold water. Return water to a boil and cook beans until crisp-tender, about 3 minutes, and transfer with slotted spoon to ice water. Drain vegetables well.

While vegetables are cooking, whisk together vinegar, mustards, and sugar and add oil in a slow stream, whisking until emulsified. Whisk in dill and salt and pepper to taste.

Serve vegetables with sauce.

BALSAMIC BEETS AND RED ONIONS
Serves 4 to 6

2   tablespoons olive oil
1   medium red onion, thinly sliced
2   (15-oz) cans small whole beets, drained and cut lengthwise into eighths
¼   cup balsamic vinegar
¼   cup fresh orange juice
2   tablespoons chopped fresh dill, or to taste
1   teaspoon sugar

Heat oil in a large nonstick skillet over moderately high heat until hot but not smoking, then sauté onion, stirring, until golden, about 6 minutes. Add beets and vinegar and simmer, stirring, until liquid is almost evaporated, about 2 minutes. Stir in orange juice, dill, sugar, and salt and pepper to taste.

SPICY COLLARD GREENS
Serves 6

¼   lb sliced bacon, halved crosswise
1   large onion, chopped
1   large fresh jalapeño chile, seeded if desired and chopped
½   cup chicken broth
3   tablespoons cider vinegar
1   tablespoon dark brown sugar, or to taste
2   lb collard greens (preferably with small leaves), coarse stems and ribs discarded and leaves coarsely chopped

Cook bacon in a deep heavy pot over moderate heat until crisp and transfer to paper towels to drain, reserving drippings in pot. Cook onion and jalapeño in drippings over moderate heat, stirring, until softened. Add broth, vinegar, and sugar and simmer, stirring until sugar is dissolved, about 1 minute. Add collard greens and simmer, covered, stirring occasionally, until tender, about 15 minutes. Season with salt and pepper.

Serve collards topped with bacon.

QUICK grains

It seems like only yesterday that American epicureans returned from Italy with tales of creamy polenta (cornmeal) and risotto (Arborio rice). While these grains have slowly but surely been assimilated, our desire for new, unusual grains continues. In recent years, aromatic rices appeared from Thailand (jasmine rice) as well as from India (basmati rice); and it turns out that quinoa—the crunchy, mild, sweet-flavored seeds that are gaining in popularity—is indigenous to the high valleys of the Peruvian Andes. Using these and other quick-cooking grains, we've developed a handful of seductive side dishes—the perfect complement to our grills and stove-top recipes.

HERBED JASMINE RICE

Serves 2

Here we've cooked the rice like pasta—a method that can be applied to any long-grain rice (preferably not converted). As for the fresh herbs, we used lemon thyme and chives, but take advantage of whatever you have on hand.

¾ cup jasmine rice
1 tablespoon unsalted butter
¼ cup chopped mixed fresh herbs

Cook rice in a 3-quart saucepan of boiling salted water, stirring occasionally, until tender, 10 to 15 minutes, and drain. Toss rice with butter and herbs and season with salt and pepper.

Photo on page 147

QUINOA WITH TARRAGON AND SUGAR SNAP PEAS

Serves 6

1 cup quinoa
½ lb sugar snap peas, trimmed
1 tablespoon fresh lemon juice
2 teaspoons extra-virgin olive oil
1 to 2 tablespoons finely chopped fresh tarragon

Wash quinoa in at least 5 changes cold water, rubbing grains and letting them settle before pouring off most water, until water runs clear and drain in a fine sieve.

Blanch peas in a 4- to 5-quart saucepan of boiling water 30 seconds and transfer with a slotted spoon to a bowl. Return water to a boil and cook quinoa 10 minutes. Drain in sieve and rinse under cold water. Set sieve over a saucepan of boiling water and steam quinoa, covered with a clean kitchen towel and lid, until fluffy and dry, 10 to 12 minutes.

While quinoa is steaming, cut sugar snap peas into ½-inch pieces.

Whisk together lemon juice and oil in a large bowl and add quinoa, peas, tarragon to taste, and salt and pepper to taste, tossing to combine.

Each serving about 137 calories and 3 grams fat

COOKING AND HANDLING
RICE AND GRAINS

Rice is cultivated on every inhabited continent and consumed daily by more than half of the world's population. It is no wonder, then, that thousands of different strains exist. A particular variety can be recognized by the length of its grain, by its color, and by its relative "stickiness" when cooked.

Usually, the variety itself determines the manner in which the rice is cooked, but cultural habit often plays a role. Sometimes, too, a little experimenting proves that there are alternatives. Recently, *Gourmet*'s cooks discovered that jasmine rice (usually cooked by the common absorption method) can be simply boiled and drained in a fraction of the time with great results.

Uncooked white rice keeps for a long time when stored in a cool, dry place, away from direct sunlight. Brown and black rices, however, are unmilled and have layers of bran and germ that can become rancid. These should be stored in sealed containers in the refrigerator. All leftover cooked rice should also be refrigerated in an airtight container.

Beyond rice, a variety of other whole and processed grains exists. Whole grains, with their bran and germ layers intact, are the healthiest choice, but these generally take a long time to cook. Luckily, some processed grains, like grits, cook quickly, and bulgur, made from steamed and cracked wheat berries, often just requires a bit of a soak. Whole grains can become rancid if exposed to heat or light, so they are best purchased from a shop with high turnover. Store whole grains, refrigerated, in airtight containers. Processed grains can be kept longer, preferably in a cool, dry place away from direct sunlight.

—Diane Keitt

RISOTTO MILANESE

Serves 4

3   cups chicken broth
1   cup water
1   small onion, finely chopped
3   tablespoons unsalted butter
1½ cups Arborio rice
¼   cup freshly grated parmesan
¼   teaspoon crumbled saffron threads

Bring broth and water to a simmer in a saucepan and keep at a bare simmer.

Cook onion in 2 tablespoons butter in a 3-quart heavy saucepan over moderate heat, stirring occasionally, until softened. Add rice, stirring to coat. Add 1 cup simmering broth mixture and cook, stirring constantly and keeping at a simmer, until absorbed. Continue cooking rice at a simmer and adding broth mixture, about ½ cup at a time, stirring constantly and letting each addition be absorbed before adding next, until rice is tender and creamy-looking but still al dente, about 18 minutes total. (There may be broth mixture left over.) Stir in parmesan, saffron, remaining tablespoon butter, and salt and pepper to taste and cook over low heat until heated through, about 3 minutes.

Photo below

BASMATI AND CUMIN PILAF

Serves 6

1   cup white basmati rice
¼   cup finely chopped shallot
1¼   teaspoons cumin seeds, toasted
1   teaspoon olive oil
1   tablespoon minced peeled fresh ginger
½   cup low-fat chicken broth
1   cup water
2   tablespoons chopped salted cashews

Rinse rice in several changes of water until water runs clear and drain well in a sieve. Cook shallot and cumin in oil in a 2-quart heavy saucepan over moderately high heat, stirring, until shallot is golden. Stir in rice and ginger and cook, stirring, 1 minute. Add broth and water and bring to a boil, uncovered. Cook pilaf over very low heat, covered, until rice is tender and liquid is absorbed, about 13 minutes. Remove pan from heat and let rice stand, undisturbed, 5 minutes. Fluff with a fork and stir in cashews and salt and pepper to taste.

Each serving about 137 calories and 2 grams fat

CARAWAY RICE CAKES

Serves 2

1 cup water
¾ cup chicken broth
¾ cup long-grain white rice
1 teaspoon caraway seeds
¼ teaspoon salt
1 tablespoon unsalted butter, melted

Bring water, broth, rice, caraway seeds, and salt to a boil in a 1½- to 2-quart heavy saucepan and cook, covered, over very low heat until liquid is absorbed and rice is tender, about 20 minutes.

Preheat broiler and butter a baking sheet.

Fluff rice with a fork. Fill a ⅓-cup measure with rice, packing it, and turn out onto baking sheet. Make 5 more rice cakes in same manner, arranging about 3 inches apart on baking sheet. Gently flatten cakes with back of a fork to 4 inches in diameter and cool 5 minutes. Brush cakes with melted butter and broil 3 to 4 inches from heat until pale golden, about 4 minutes.

HERBED BULGUR WITH APRICOTS

Serves 4

Bulgur is often packaged and sold as tabbouleh. We use Near East tabbouleh mix, available at most supermarkets. Simply discard the accompanying seasoning pouch.

¾ cup medium bulgur
2 tablespoons finely chopped dried apricots
1 teaspoon kosher salt
1½ cups boiling-hot water
1½ to 2 tablespoons fresh lemon juice
½ teaspoon finely grated fresh lemon zest
1 tablespoon extra-virgin olive oil
¼ cup finely chopped fresh mint
¼ cup finely chopped fresh cilantro

Stir together bulgur, apricots, kosher salt, and boiling-hot water in a bowl and let stand, covered tightly with plastic wrap, 30 minutes.

Whisk together lemon juice, zest, and oil. Drain bulgur mixture in a sieve, pressing lightly to remove as much moisture as possible, and return to bowl. Toss with dressing, mint, cilantro, and salt and pepper to taste.

Each serving about 132 calories and 4 grams fat

FRIED GRITS TRIANGLES

Serves 4 to 6

3¼ cups water
1 cup quick-cooking grits
1 cup grated sharp Cheddar
½ cup finely chopped scallions
1 large egg
1 cup fine dry bread crumbs
1⅔ cups vegetable oil

Bring 3 cups water to a boil in a 1½-quart heavy saucepan. Add grits in a stream, whisking, and cook, covered, over moderately low heat, whisking occasionally, 5 minutes, or until thickened. Add cheese, scallions, and salt and pepper to taste, stirring, until cheese is melted. Spread grits in an 8-inch square baking pan and set pan in a larger pan of ice water to chill grits until firm, about 10 minutes.

Cut grits into 4 squares and cut each square into 4 triangles. Beat together egg and remaining ¼ cup water in a bowl and season bread crumbs with salt and pepper in a large shallow baking pan. Lift triangles carefully out of pan with an offset spatula or a fork. Dip triangles in egg, letting excess drip off, and dredge in bread crumbs.

Heat oil in a 12-inch deep skillet over moderately high heat until a drop of water sizzles when added. Fry triangles in 3 batches until golden, carefully turning with 2 spatulas, about 1 minute on each side. Drain on paper towels and serve warm.

CRUNCHY VEGETABLE AND BROWN RICE SALAD

Serves 4

½ cup short-grain brown rice
1 medium zucchini (½ lb), cut into ¼-inch dice
2 celery ribs, cut into ¼-inch dice
1 carrot, cut into ¼-inch dice
1 yellow bell pepper, cut into ¼-inch dice
2 tablespoons fresh lemon juice
¼ cup chicken broth
1 tablespoon coarse-grained mustard
1 tablespoon olive oil
½ teaspoon salt
¼ teaspoon freshly ground black pepper
½ bunch arugula (4 oz), tough stems removed and leaves chopped
4 scallions, chopped

Cook rice in a 2-quart saucepan three fourths full of boiling salted water, uncovered, stirring occasionally, until al dente, about 25 minutes. Drain rice and rinse under cold running water until cool. Drain well.

Have ready a bowl of ice and cold water. Blanch zucchini, celery, carrot, and bell pepper in a saucepan of boiling salted water 1 minute. Drain vegetables in a sieve and transfer to ice water to stop cooking. Drain well.

Whisk together lemon juice, broth, mustard, oil, salt, and pepper in a large bowl. Add rice, blanched vegetables, arugula, scallions, and salt and pepper to taste and toss. Serve salad at room temperature.

Each serving about 158 calories and 5 grams fat

Photo opposite

CREAMY PARMESAN POLENTA

Serves 4

This easy side dish pairs perfectly with our pork chops with coriander-cumin spice rub (recipe on page 65).

3 cups water
¾ cup instant polenta
¾ to 1 cup freshly grated Parmigiano-Reggiano
1 tablespoon unsalted butter

Bring water to a boil in a 2-quart saucepan and slowly add polenta, whisking constantly. Cook polenta over moderate heat, whisking constantly, 5 minutes. Remove from heat and whisk in cheese, butter, and salt and pepper to taste. Serve immediately.

Photo on page 64

FOOLPROOF LONG-GRAIN RICE

Serves 6

The following method is our favorite way to cook long-grain rice—we love the consistency it yields. We learned the technique from some of our Latino and Louisianian colleagues.

3 cups water
1½ cups long-grain rice (not converted)
1¼ teaspoons salt

Stir together all ingredients in a 2½- to 3-quart heavy saucepan and boil, uncovered, until steam holes appear in rice and grains on surface appear dry, about 8 minutes. Cover pan and cook rice over very low heat 15 minutes more. Remove pan from heat and let rice stand, covered, 5 minutes.

Fluff rice with a fork before serving.

QUICK green salaDs

Those who care about eating well try to include a salad with dinner, even on weeknights. And yet most of us, night after night, get into the habit of just mixing green lettuces with a bit of olive oil and balsamic or red-wine vinegar. Well, it's never too late to turn a new leaf! Here's a newly developed collection of inspired salads and dressings, including fabulous make-ahead recipes for an everyday salad mix and vinaigrette. We've even included a few favorites that usually only appear in restaurants, like ginger miso vinaigrette and guacamole salad dressing, along with plenty of sensational low-fat options.

DANDELION SALAD WITH WARM HAZELNUT VINAIGRETTE

Serves 6

Dandelions are now cultivated commercially and are widely available at farmers markets and supermarkets. Great additions to this salad are red onion and shaved parmesan.

2   large bunches dandelion greens (2 lb), tough stems discarded
3   garlic cloves, finely chopped
¼   cup hazelnuts, coarsely chopped
2   tablespoons extra-virgin olive oil
1   tablespoon balsamic vinegar

Cut top 5 inches from greens and reserve. Cut remaining greens into ¾-inch slices. Put all greens in a large serving bowl.

Cook garlic and nuts in oil in a small heavy skillet over moderate heat, stirring, until garlic is golden. Stir in vinegar and salt and pepper to taste. Pour hot vinaigrette over greens and toss to combine.

Photo on page 155

ENDIVE, STILTON, AND BACON SALAD

Serves 2

This salad yields generous portions. Combined with a loaf of crusty bread, it's easily a meal in itself.

3   tablespoons extra-virgin olive oil
1   tablespoon fresh lemon juice
4   endives (1 lb), cut into ¾-inch pieces
2   oz Stilton, crumbled
¼   cup fresh flat-leaf parsley
4   bacon slices, cooked crisp and drained on paper towels

Whisk together oil, lemon juice, and salt and pepper to taste in a large bowl. Add endives, Stilton, and parsley and toss to coat. Crumble bacon over salad.

Photo opposite

SESAME, CUCUMBER, AND WATERCRESS SALAD

Serves 4

1   (¾-lb) English cucumber, halved lengthwise, seeded, and cut crosswise into ¼-inch-thick slices
½   bunch watercress, tough stems discarded
1   tablespoon seasoned rice vinegar
2   teaspoons sesame seeds, toasted
1   teaspoon Asian sesame oil
¼   teaspoon dried hot red pepper flakes

Toss together all ingredients with salt to taste.

Each serving about 29 calories and 2 grams fat

ARUGULA-PARSLEY SALAD WITH CHICKPEAS, PICKLES, AND SHERRY-MUSTARD VINAIGRETTE

Serves 2

½	red onion, thinly sliced
2	cups loosely packed arugula (2 oz), coarse stems discarded
2	teaspoons extra-virgin olive oil
2	teaspoons Sherry vinegar
1½	teaspoons Dijon mustard
½	cup drained canned chickpeas (3 oz), rinsed and skins removed
1	vine-ripened tomato, seeded and cut into ¼-inch dice
2	dill pickles (each 2¾ inches long), cut into ¼-inch dice
1	cup fresh flat-leaf parsley

Cover onion with cold water in a bowl and soak 20 minutes. Drain and pat dry. Tear arugula into bite-size pieces. Whisk together oil, vinegar, mustard, and salt and pepper to taste.

Toss together onion, arugula, chickpeas, tomato, pickle, parsley, vinaigrette, and salt and pepper to taste.

Each serving about 175 calories and 6 grams fat

Photo right, top

SESAME SPINACH AND BEET SALAD

Serves 2

- 2 medium beets (10 oz)
- 1 bunch spinach (¾ lb), stems discarded and leaves cut into ⅓-inch strips
- 4 teaspoons rice vinegar
- 1 teaspoon soy sauce
- ½ teaspoon Asian sesame oil
- ¼ teaspoon sugar

GARNISH:
toasted sesame seeds

Peel beets and very thinly slice with a sharp thin knife or a *mandoline*. Cut beet slices into fine julienne strips and transfer to a bowl with spinach.

Stir together vinegar, soy sauce, oil, and sugar in a small bowl, stirring until sugar is dissolved. Toss spinach and beets with vinaigrette.

Photo opposite, bottom

MUSTARD GREENS WITH CITRUS JUICE AND DATES

Serves 4

Be sure to use only tender mustard greens for this salad—large, thick leaves will be tough.

- ½ cup pitted dates, chopped
- 2 tablespoons fresh orange juice
- 1 tablespoon fresh lemon juice
- 4 cups tender mustard leaves, trimmed, center rib discarded, and chopped
- 1 tablespoon extra-virgin olive oil

Stir together dates and citrus juices in a large bowl. Toss with greens, oil, and salt and pepper to taste.

Each serving about 120 calories and 4 grams fat

LOW-FAT CHOPPED SALAD

Serves 6

FOR DRESSING
- 2 tablespoons apricot preserves
- 2 tablespoons fresh lime juice
- 1 tablespoon fresh orange juice
- ½ teaspoon dried hot red pepper flakes

- ½ lb *jícama*, peeled and cut into ⅓-inch dice
- ¼ lb seedless cucumber, cut into ⅓-inch dice
- 1 red bell pepper, cut into ⅓-inch dice
- ½ cup chopped red onion
- 4 cups shredded romaine
- 1 cup radish sprouts
- ⅓ cup chopped fresh cilantro
- 1½ teaspoons cumin seeds, toasted

MAKE DRESSING:
Purée dressing ingredients in a blender.

Just before serving, toss all remaining ingredients with dressing and salt and pepper to taste.

Each serving about 55 calories and less than 1 gram fat

HOW TO CHOP an onion

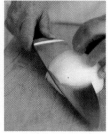

So many of our recipes call for chopped onions, we figured a refresher course might be in order. (No, you really can't use the food processor—you'll end up with a combination of onion slush and chunks.) Always start with a sharp knife. In the test kitchens, we hone our knives at least once a day; some of us with each use. Choose a knife with a wide blade; that way, its own weight will do most of the work.

Prep the onion: When you peel it, remove the leathery outermost layer just under the papery skin as well as the sheer, sticky membrane; the outer layer will never become tender, and the sheer one can cause your knife to slip. Cut off the tip of the blossom end but leave the root end intact. Next, beginning at the root end, cut the onion in half—the point here being that round things roll, flat things don't.

Chop the onion: Holding the knife parallel to the cutting board and starting at the blossom end, make several even, parallel cuts into the onion, stopping short of the root end. (The root end both keeps the onion layers together and gives you a kind of button to hold on to as you work.) Still avoiding the root end, make even, parallel cuts perpendicular to the board. Then, starting at the blossom end again, slice across the cuts you just made, watch chopped onion begin to appear, and keep slicing all the way over to the root button, which you can now discard. (When chopping, curl the fingers holding the onion to protect them.)

—Zanne Stewart

GREEN BEAN, ASIAN PEAR, AND RADICCHIO SALAD

Serves 6

Admittedly, the only salad "green" here is a touch of fresh mint, but every salad chapter, we feel, should include radicchio. We've paired it with green beans and Asian pear to add crunch and a bit of sweetness.

¾ lb *haricots verts* or thin green beans, trimmed

FOR DRESSING
2½ tablespoons fresh lemon juice
4 tablespoons extra-virgin olive oil
1 teaspoon sugar
½ teaspoon anise seeds

1 Asian pear*, cut into thin wedges, then chopped
1 medium head radicchio, shredded
2 tablespoons coarsely chopped fresh mint

available at Asian markets and some supermarkets

Cook beans in a large saucepan of boiling salted water until just tender, 3 to 4 minutes. Drain and rinse with cold water to cool.

MAKE DRESSING:
While beans are cooking, purée dressing ingredients in a blender.

Toss together beans, pear, radicchio, mint, dressing, and salt and pepper to taste.

CHICORY SALAD WITH WALNUTS AND GOAT CHEESE

Serves 4

½ cup walnuts, chopped
3 tablespoons olive oil
¼ cup soft mild fresh goat cheese (2 oz)
1 tablespoon fresh lemon juice
2 tablespoons water
1 red apple such as Gala
5 cups chicory, chopped

Cook walnuts in oil in a 10-inch skillet over moderate heat until a few shades darker, 2 to 3 minutes. Cool.

Whisk together goat cheese, lemon juice, water, and pepper to taste in a large bowl until goat cheese is smooth. Cut apple into ½-inch pieces and add to goat cheese with walnuts and chicory. Toss to coat.

MIZUNA, CHOPPED PARMESAN, AND RED BEAN SALAD

Serves 4

1 tablespoon fresh lemon juice
½ teaspoon Dijon mustard
½ teaspoon salt
3 tablespoons extra-virgin olive oil
5 cups *mizuna* or mixed baby greens
1 (14½-oz) can pinto or red beans, rinsed and drained
¼ large sweet onion such as Vidalia, cut lengthwise into thin wedges (½ cup)
1 (3-oz) piece parmesan, chopped fine (⅓ cup)

Whisk together lemon juice, mustard, and salt in a large bowl, then whisk in oil. Add *mizuna*, beans, onion, and parmesan and toss to coat.

EVERYDAY SALAD

Makes about 16 salads

Having a ready-made salad at your fingertips makes everyday cooking a breeze. This easy recipe yields 16 side salads that will keep for about a week. (Recipe may be halved.) A host of salad dressings—including our new favorite, everyday vinaigrette—follows.

- 1   (³⁄₄-lb) head red-leaf lettuce
- 1   (³⁄₄-lb) head curly-leaf green lettuce
- 2   bunches arugula (4 cups)
- ½   lb carrots, coarsely grated

Discard any wilted lettuce or arugula leaves. Wash greens in batches in a large bowl of cold water and dry with a salad spinner. Do not tear lettuce or arugula leaves.

Put a length of 3 connected paper towels on a work surface and arrange one quarter of greens on top. Sprinkle with one quarter of carrots. Gently roll up paper towels and put bundle in a sealable plastic bag, pressing gently to remove excess air. Repeat with remaining greens and carrots.

To serve, tear leaves into bite-size pieces and toss with your favorite salad dressing and salt and pepper to taste.

EVERYDAY VINAIGRETTE

Makes about 2½ cups

This versatile dressing is good on most varieties of lettuce. It keeps, covered and chilled, 1 week.

- ½   cup red-wine vinegar
- ½   cup freshly grated parmesan
- ⅓   cup water
- 1½ tablespoons Dijon mustard
- 1½ teaspoons sugar
- 1½ teaspoons salt
- 1   large garlic clove
- 1½ cups olive oil
- ⅓   cup fresh flat-leaf parsley

Purée vinegar, cheese, water, mustard, sugar, salt, and garlic in a blender. Add oil and parsley and purée until parsley is finely chopped.

LOW-FAT THOUSAND ISLAND DRESSING

Makes about 1 cup

Pair this dressing with crisp lettuce. Sliced tomatoes and seafood salad are other natural pairings.

- ⅓   cup low-fat mayonnaise
- 2   tablespoons ketchup
- 2   tablespoons fresh lemon juice
- 2   tablespoons minced red bell pepper
- 1   tablespoon minced onion
- 1   tablespoon minced fresh flat-leaf parsley
- 1   tablespoon sweet pickle relish
     Pinch of cayenne
- ¼   cup water

Blend all ingredients and salt to taste in a blender or food processor until smooth, adding up to 2 tablespoons additional water if necessary to thin to desired consistency.

Each tablespoon about 12 calories and less than 1 gram fat

Photo opposite

LOW-FAT BACON MUSTARD DRESSING

Makes about 1 cup

Serve this dressing with crisp lettuce. It is also delicious with sliced tomatoes or potato salad.

1	teaspoon finely chopped uncooked bacon (about ¼ slice)
6	tablespoons fresh orange juice
½	cup nonfat sour cream
1½	tablespoons fresh lemon juice
1	tablespoon Dijon mustard
3	tablespoons chopped scallion (white part only)
1	large garlic clove, minced
1	teaspoon brown sugar

Cook bacon in a small heavy skillet over moderate heat, stirring, until crisp and remove from heat. Add orange juice, stirring and scraping up brown bits. Blend bacon mixture, remaining ingredients, and salt and pepper to taste in a blender until smooth.

Each tablespoon about 14 calories and less than 1 gram fat

Photo on page 162

LOW-FAT HERBED RANCH DRESSING

Makes about 1 cup

Try this dressing with soft lettuce. It also complements shellfish salad or salmon salad.

¾	cup well-shaken low-fat (1½%) buttermilk
2	tablespoons low-fat mayonnaise
2	tablespoons nonfat sour cream
1	tablespoon fresh basil, minced
1	tablespoon finely chopped fresh chives
2	teaspoons cider vinegar
1	teaspoon dry mustard
1	teaspoon fresh thyme
1	garlic clove, minced
½	teaspoon sugar

Blend all ingredients and salt and pepper to taste in a blender or food processor until smooth.

Each tablespoon about 12 calories and less than 1 gram fat

Photo on page 162

LOW-FAT CHIPOTLE CHUTNEY DRESSING

Makes about 1 cup

Serve this dressing with soft lettuce. Alternatively, try potato salad or fresh fruit such as honeydew melon, apples, or oranges.

¼ cup Major Grey's chutney
¼ cup fresh orange juice
1 tablespoon fresh lime juice
2 tablespoons water
1 teaspoon minced canned *chipotle* chile in *adobo* sauce*
1 teaspoon ground cumin
1 garlic clove, minced

available at Hispanic markets, some specialty foods shops, and by mail order from Adriana's Caravan, (800) 316-0820

Blend all ingredients and salt to taste in a blender until smooth.

Each tablespoon about 16 calories and less than 1 gram fat

Photo on page 162

CHUTNEY GARLIC DRESSING

Makes about 1 cup

¼ cup Major Grey's chutney
½ teaspoon dried hot red pepper flakes
2 tablespoons fresh lemon juice
⅓ cup water
2 large garlic cloves, chopped
½ cup vegetable oil

Blend together chutney, red pepper flakes, lemon juice, water, garlic, and salt to taste in a blender until smooth. With motor running, add oil in a stream and blend until emulsified.

Photo below

SOY-SESAME VINAIGRETTE
Makes about ¾ cup

Serve on romaine or other crisp-leaf green lettuce.

¼   cup seasoned rice vinegar
2   tablespoons soy sauce
1   tablespoon water
2   scallions, chopped
½   teaspoon minced garlic
¼   teaspoon dried hot red pepper flakes
¼   cup olive oil
1   tablespoon sesame oil

Whisk together vinegar, soy sauce, water, scallions, garlic, and red pepper flakes. Add oils in a slow stream and whisk until emulsified.

GUACAMOLE DRESSING
Makes about 1¾ cups

Serve on romaine or other crisp-leaf green lettuce.

1   medium ripe California avocado, peeled and pitted
½   cup water
⅓   cup olive oil
¼   cup fresh lemon juice
½   cup fresh cilantro
1   fresh jalapeño chile, seeded
1   small garlic clove
¾   teaspoon salt
½   teaspoon ground cumin

Purée all ingredients in a blender and season with salt and pepper to taste.

GINGER-MISO VINAIGRETTE
Makes about ⅓ cup

To make ginger juice, grate peeled fresh ginger onto cheesecloth, gather cloth into a bundle, and squeeze out juice. Or you can squeeze pieces of ginger in a garlic press. This dressing is good on Boston lettuce or other delicate greens.

2   tablespoons rice vinegar (not seasoned)
1   tablespoon ginger juice (see above)
1   tablespoon *shiro miso* (white fermented-soybean paste)
1   teaspoon sugar
3   tablespoons olive oil

Whisk together vinegar, ginger juice, *miso*, and sugar, whisking until sugar is dissolved. Add oil in a slow stream, whisking until emulsified.

salad mix-ins

Rest assured, none of *Gourmet*'s food editors would serve a humdrum, same-old-story salad, even on a weeknight. When we asked how they embellish their own salads, we were inundated with splendid ideas, including the following:

- Homemade croutons made with leftover bread, preferably peasant or whole-grain (the better the bread, the better the croutons): Cut the bread into crouton-size cubes and freeze; then whenever you want croutons, toss the frozen cubes quickly in a bit of olive oil, season with sea salt, and bake in a 350°F oven until crisp.

- Slivered fennel and shaved Parmigiano-Reggiano

- Sliced ripe pears and crumbled blue cheese

- Raisins and toasted sunflower seeds

- Sliced figs (fresh or dried) and goat cheese

- Crumbled feta and chopped black olives (preferably Kalamata or Niçoise)

- Sliced apple, crumbled sharp Cheddar, and bacon

- Sliced cooked beets and toasted walnuts

- Roasted red peppers, canned white beans (rinsed and drained), and fresh whole basil leaves

- Sprouts and toasted pumpkin seeds

- Sliced red onion and orange sections

- Crisp-fried thin slices of shallots or garlic with fresh mint leaves

- Capers (rinsed and drained), flaked tuna, and fresh flat-leaf parsley

- Corn, canned black beans (rinsed and drained), and fresh cilantro leaves

—Ellen Morrissey

QUICK snacks

Even when time is tight and *everyone* wants dinner, it's nice to take a moment to decompress and completely relax. Savor a little nibble. Pour a glass of wine. Take a deep breath. Here we offer more than a dozen quick bites that'll see you through until you sit down to dinner, even if dinner cooks in record time. But be very careful—with absolutely addictive snacks like our sweet potato chips, crab canapés, and *jícama* sticks—you just might ruin your appetite.

SWEET-POTATO CHIPS WITH LIME SALT

Serves 2

4   limes
½   teaspoon salt
1   large sweet potato (¾ lb), peeled
3   cups vegetable oil

Finely grate enough lime zest to measure
½ teaspoon and stir together with salt in a
cup. Shave as many long strips as possible
from potato using a vegetable peeler.

Heat oil in a deep 10-inch heavy skillet over
moderately high heat until a deep-fat thermometer registers 375°F and fry potato strips
in 3 batches, stirring frequently, until lightly
browned and bubbling stops, about 1 minute.
Transfer chips with a slotted spoon to paper
towels to drain and sprinkle with lime salt.
Recipe can be doubled to serve 4.

Photo on page 169

SWISS CHEESE WITH WALNUTS AND MUSTARD

Makes about 2½ cups

3   tablespoons Dijon mustard
3   tablespoons sour cream
¼   teaspoon dried tarragon, crumbled
½   cup thinly sliced scallion
2½ cups coarsely grated Swiss (½ lb)
½   cup chopped walnuts, toasted and cooled

ACCOMPANIMENT:
crackers

Whisk together mustard, sour cream, tarragon,
scallion, and pepper to taste. Stir in cheese
and walnuts.

Photo right, top

CHICKPEA, GARLIC, AND PARSLEY DIP

Makes about 2 cups

2	garlic cloves, chopped
½	teaspoon salt
1	(19-oz) can chickpeas (2 cups), rinsed and drained
½	cup fresh flat-leaf parsley
¼	cup water
3	tablespoons fresh lemon juice
¼	cup extra-virgin olive oil

ACCOMPANIMENT:
toasted pita wedges or toasted French bread slices

Mash garlic and salt to a paste. Blend garlic paste and remaining ingredients except oil in a food processor until smooth. With motor running, add oil in a slow stream. Season with salt.

Photo opposite, bottom

CREAMY CLAM DIP

Makes about 2 cups

8	oz cream cheese, softened
¼	cup sour cream
2	(6½-oz) cans minced clams, drained, reserving 3 tablespoons liquid
⅓	cup finely chopped red bell pepper
1	shallot, minced
2	tablespoons minced fresh flat-leaf parsley
¾	teaspoon Worcestershire sauce
⅛	teaspoon cayenne

ACCOMPANIMENT:
toasted pita wedges or potato chips

Whisk together cream cheese and sour cream in a bowl until smooth. Stir in remaining ingredients and salt to taste.

Photo opposite, bottom

RED PEPPER DIP WITH WALNUTS

Makes about 1½ cups

1	small onion, chopped
2	large garlic cloves, sliced
¼	cup olive oil
1	(12-oz) jar roasted red peppers (1¾ cups), rinsed and drained
½	cup walnuts, toasted and cooled
⅓	cup fresh basil
1	slice homemade-type sandwich bread, chopped
2	tablespoons fresh lemon juice

ACCOMPANIMENT:
toasted pita wedges

Cook onion and garlic in oil in a skillet over moderate heat, stirring, until softened. Blend remaining ingredients in a food processor until nuts are chopped fine. With motor running, gradually add onion mixture and blend until incorporated. Season with salt.

Photo opposite, bottom

BRUSCHETTA WITH WHITE BEANS AND WALNUTS
Makes 6 *bruschette*

2   garlic cloves
1   (15- to 16-oz) can white beans,
    rinsed and drained
1½ teaspoons fresh lemon juice
¼   cup extra-virgin olive oil
6   (¼-inch-thick) slices rustic
    Italian bread, toasted
⅓   cup walnuts, toasted and coarsely
    chopped

GARNISH:
chopped fresh flat-leaf parsley

Mince garlic in a food processor and purée
with beans, lemon juice, and 1 tablespoon
oil until smooth.

Drizzle toasts with 2 tablespoons oil. Divide
purée among toasts and top with nuts. Drizzle
remaining tablespoon oil over *bruschetta*.

Photo below

CHICKPEA CUMIN DIP
Makes about 3 cups

We love this reduced-fat version of hummus.

1   (19-oz) can chickpeas (2 cups),
    rinsed and drained
12 oz soft tofu, drained
1   tablespoon cumin seeds, toasted
3   tablespoons fresh lemon juice,
    or to taste
1   tablespoon extra-virgin olive oil
¼   cup chopped fresh flat-leaf parsley

GARNISH:
chopped fresh flat-leaf parsley

ACCOMPANIMENT:
pita toasts and/or crudités

Purée chickpeas, tofu, cumin seeds, lemon
juice, and oil in a food processor. Stir in
parsley and salt and pepper to taste.

Each serving (¼ cup) about 88 calories
and 4 grams fat

Photo below

FENNEL PITA TOASTS

Serves 4

- ¼ teaspoon fennel seeds
- 1 (6-inch) pita loaf (preferably pocketless)
- 1 teaspoon extra-virgin olive oil
- ⅛ teaspoon coarse kosher salt

Preheat oven to 350°F.

Lightly crush fennel seeds on a cutting board with side of a knife. Brush top of pita with oil and sprinkle with crushed fennel and kosher salt. Bake on a baking sheet in middle of oven until golden and crisp, about 3 minutes. Cut pita into 4 wedges.

Each wedge about 37 calories and 1 gram fat

TOASTED SPICED PUMPKIN SEEDS

Serves 6 to 8

- 1 tablespoon olive oil
- 2 cups hulled green pumpkin seeds*
- 1½ teaspoons ground cumin
- ¼ teaspoon cayenne, or to taste

*available at natural foods stores

Heat oil in a seasoned cast-iron skillet or large heavy skillet over moderately high heat until hot but not smoking, then cook pumpkin seeds with salt to taste, stirring constantly, until they are puffed and golden and make popping noises, about 7 minutes. Stir in cumin and cayenne and cook 1 minute more. Transfer seeds to a shallow plate and cool slightly.

PARSNIP SHOESTRING CRISPS

Makes about ¾ pound

- 2 lb parsnips, scrubbed
  Vegetable oil for deep-frying
- 1 tablespoon celery salt
- 1½ teaspoons dried dill, crumbled
- ¼ teaspoon freshly ground black pepper

Cut parsnips lengthwise into fine julienne strips in a food processor fitted with fine julienne disk.

Heat 1½ inches oil in a heavy pot over moderately high heat until a deep-fat thermometer registers 375°F and fry parsnips, a handful at a time, until golden brown, about 1 minute. Transfer with a slotted spoon to paper towels to drain. Combine celery salt, dill, and pepper and sprinkle over parsnip crisps.

SPICY POPCORN WITH PARMESAN

Serves 4

- 1 (¼-lb) piece parmesan
- ½ cup popcorn kernels
- ½ tablespoon extra-virgin olive oil
- ⅛ teaspoon cayenne, or to taste

Grate enough parmesan on small teardrop holes of a hand-held grater to measure ½ cup. Pop popcorn in a hot-air corn popper and immediately toss with cheese, oil, cayenne, and salt to taste.

Each serving about 151 calories and 5 grams fat

SUN-DRIED TOMATO AND ROASTED RED PEPPER DIP

Makes about 2¼ cups

1   garlic clove
    Pinch of salt
2   (7-oz) jars roasted red peppers,
    drained and patted dry
8   sun-dried tomato halves, soaked in hot water
    5 minutes, drained well, and patted dry
1   tablespoon fresh lemon juice
2   tablespoons chopped fresh flat-leaf parsley
4   oz cream cheese, cut into bits and softened
½   cup sour cream

GARNISH:
chopped fresh flat-leaf parsley

ACCOMPANIMENT:
lightly toasted pita triangles or crudités

Mash garlic and salt to a paste. Purée garlic paste, peppers, tomatoes, lemon juice, and parsley in a food processor. Add cream cheese, sour cream, and salt and pepper to taste, and purée, scraping down side of bowl occasionally, until smooth.

Photo below

LIGHT CRAB CANAPÉS ON CUMIN PITA TOASTS

Serves 8

1   tablespoon olive oil
1   tablespoon dark Asian sesame oil
2   teaspoons ground cumin
4   (6-inch) pitas with pockets, halved horizontally
½   lb jumbo lump crab meat, picked over
3   tablespoons low-fat sour cream
2   tablespoons finely chopped scallions
2   tablespoons finely chopped fresh cilantro
1   tablespoon fresh lime juice, or to taste
    Dash of Tabasco

Preheat oven to 425°F.

Stir together oils, cumin, and salt and pepper to taste and brush on cut sides of pitas. Cut each pita half into 8 wedges and arrange, cut sides up, on a large baking sheet. Bake pitas in middle of oven until edges are crisp, about 10 minutes. Transfer to a rack to cool (and crisp).

Stir together crab meat with remaining ingredients and salt and pepper to taste.

Top each toast with some crab meat.

Each serving about 176 calories and 5 grams fat

JÍCAMA STICKS WITH CILANTRO AND LIME

Serves 4

1½ lb *jícama*, peeled and cut into
    2- by ¼-inch sticks
¼   cup chopped fresh cilantro
2   tablespoons chopped fresh mint
2   tablespoons fresh lime juice, or to taste

Toss together all ingredients and season with salt and pepper.

Each serving about 67 calories and 0 grams fat

a snack pantry

All good cooks have a trick or two up their sleeves when it comes to creating last-minute snacks and hors d'ouevres. When we asked our *Gourmet* colleagues to reveal the contents of their home pantries, their answers included some wonderful surprises:

In bottles: Pickled okra, pickled beets, pickled Vidalia onions, *cornichons*, hot pepper jelly, Asian chili paste, roasted red peppers, olive paste, anchovies
In cans: beans (chickpeas, black beans, white beans, pinto beans—all must be rinsed and drained), artichoke hearts, *chipotle* peppers in *adobo*, tuna in oil, clams, smoked oysters
In tubes: Swedish cod roe, anchovy paste, sun-dried tomato paste
Nuts/seeds: walnuts, almonds, pecans, hazelnuts, pumpkin seeds (all refrigerated)
Crackers/breads: Carr's wholemeal biscuits, pita bread, *grissini*, tortillas (corn and flour)
Cheese: cream cheese, goat cheese, a wedge of Parmigiano-Reggiano
Dried fruits: figs, apricots, raisins, dates
From the freezer: edamame (soybeans in the pod), puff pastry, Chinese pot stickers and dumplings, pierogi (Eastern European dumplings)

Kemp Minifie, *Gourmet*'s Senior Food Editor, keeps a box of Carr's wholemeal biscuits on hand, because they're "terrific with goat cheese." Food editor Lori Powell, another fan of goat cheese and crackers, ups the ante by adding a few julienne strips of pickled beets. She often tops *croûtes* with cream cheese and pickled Vidalia onions or with roast beef and hot pepper jelly, and spreads flatbread and rye crisps with Swedish cod roe.

Any of the canned beans may be quickly seasoned and mashed into an instant spread. You can turn up the heat by adding mashed *chipotle* pepper, cumin, and garlic. Spread this spicy paste on a tortilla, top it with thin slices of roasted red pepper and chopped cilantro, roll the tortilla up, and slice into rounds for flavorful pinwheels.

Store-bought frozen puff pastry is another favorite staple—it can be quickly thawed, cut into shapes, topped with anchovy paste and grated parmesan, and baked until golden for simple, fast nibbles. Or try this quick Niçoise treat: Spread crackers with olive paste, then top with drained, flaked tuna and slivers of roasted red pepper.

—Ellen Morrissey

QUICK DESSERTS

Nothing comforts the soul after a long hard day like a homemade dessert. And yet, whether we're counting calories or simply trying to save time, we usually opt to forgo a sweet finale when preparing weeknight meals. The trick, we discovered, comes in finding absolutely scrumptious recipes (worth *every* calorie) that can be put together in minutes. A cache of such goodies follows. Several are even leaner and lighter, so you can enjoy them with an easy conscience.

COFFEE SOUFFLÉS WITH MOCHA SAUCE
Serves 2

½ cup 1% milk
2 teaspoons cornstarch
1 teaspoon instant-coffee granules
   (not espresso)
5 tablespoons granulated sugar
½ teaspoon vanilla
3 large egg whites
¼ teaspoon cream of tartar
   Confectioners sugar

ACCOMPANIMENT:
mocha sauce (recipe follows)

Whisk together milk, cornstarch, coffee granules, and 1 tablespoon granulated sugar in a small saucepan until smooth. Cook, whisking, over moderate heat until pudding boils and is thickened, 1 to 2 minutes, and transfer to a bowl. Stir in vanilla and put wax paper on surface to prevent a skin from forming. Cool pudding to warm.

Preheat oven to 400°F. Lightly oil 2 (6-oz) ramekins and sprinkle each with ½ tablespoon granulated sugar.

Beat egg whites with cream of tartar and a pinch salt in a large bowl until they just hold soft peaks. Gradually add remaining 3 tablespoons granulated sugar, beating until whites hold stiff peaks. Stir one fourth of whites into pudding to lighten and fold in remaining whites gently but thoroughly.

Mound mixture into ramekins and bake on a baking sheet in lower third of oven until puffed and golden brown, about 15 minutes. Lightly dust soufflés with confectioners sugar and serve immediately with mocha sauce.

Each serving (including sauce) about 255 calories and 5 grams fat

Photo on page 177

MOCHA SAUCE
Makes 3 tablespoons (2 servings)

2 tablespoons brewed coffee
1 oz semisweet chocolate, chopped
¼ teaspoon vanilla
⅛ teaspoon cornstarch
   Pinch of cinnamon

Cook all ingredients in a small saucepan, whisking, over moderately low heat until smooth and thickened, about 2 minutes. Remove from heat and cool to warm before serving.

Each 1½ tablespoon serving about 72 calories and 5 grams fat

Photo below

FLOURLESS CHOCOLATE CAKE

Makes 1 (8-inch) cake

4   oz fine-quality bittersweet chocolate
    (not unsweetened), chopped into
    small pieces
1   stick (½ cup) unsalted butter
¾   cup sugar
3   large eggs
½   cup unsweetened cocoa powder plus
    additional for sprinkling

Preheat oven to 375°F and butter an 8-inch
round baking pan. Line bottom with a round of
wax paper and butter paper.

Melt chocolate with butter in a double boiler or
metal bowl set over a saucepan of barely simmering water, stirring, until smooth. Remove top of
double boiler or bowl from heat and whisk sugar
into chocolate mixture. Whisk in eggs. Sift ½ cup
cocoa powder over chocolate mixture and whisk
until just combined. Pour batter into pan and
bake in middle of oven 25 minutes, or until top
has formed a thin crust. Cool in pan on a rack
5 minutes and invert onto a serving plate.

To serve, dust cake with additional cocoa powder.

BERRY COMPOTE WITH CRISPY WON TON STRIPS AND VANILLA ICE CREAM

Serves 4

*This compote makes a lovely low-fat dessert on its
own, but the contrast of creamy ice cream and
crunchy won ton makes it something special.*

FOR COMPOTE
1   cup raspberries
1   cup blackberries, halved if large
1   cup quartered strawberries
½   cup dry white wine
1   tablespoon crème de cassis or other
    blackberry liqueur
¼   cup sugar

FOR WON TON STRIPS
1   to 2 cups vegetable oil for frying
8   won ton wrappers, thawed if frozen, cut
    into ¼-inch-wide strips

1   pint super-premium ice cream

GARNISH:
confectioners sugar for dusting

MAKE COMPOTE:
Combine berries in a large bowl. Heat wine,
liqueur, and sugar in a small heavy saucepan,
stirring until sugar is dissolved, and pour over
berries. Toss gently and let stand 10 minutes.

MAKE WON TON STRIPS:
While berries are standing, heat ½ inch oil in a
medium heavy skillet over moderate heat until a
won ton sizzles when added. Fry won ton strips
in 2 or 3 batches, stirring gently with a slotted
spoon, until golden, about 30 seconds. Drain on
paper towels.

Top compote with ice cream and won tons.

CARAMELIZED FIGS WITH LEMON-YOGURT DIP

Serves 4

This lemon-yogurt dip has become our favorite sauce—low-fat or otherwise—for broiled or grilled fruit.

1   cup low-fat yogurt
1   tablespoon sour cream
      Finely grated zest from 1 lemon
3   tablespoons sugar
12   fresh figs (1½ lb), trimmed and halved

Preheat broiler and line broiling pan with a very lightly oiled sheet of foil.

Stir together yogurt, sour cream, zest, and 1½ tablespoons sugar until smooth.

Spread remaining 1½ tablespoons sugar on a small plate. Dip cut sides of figs in sugar and arrange, cut sides up, on broiling pan (for best results, arrange figs so they will be directly under flame). Broil 2 inches from flame until bubbling and caramelized, about 3 minutes.

Serve figs with dip.

Each serving about 207 calories and 3 grams fat

BROILED APPLES WITH MAPLE CALVADOS SAUCE

Serves 4

This quick dessert is like a crustless apple tart.

4   Fuji or Royal Gala apples, peeled, cored, and each cut into 16 wedges
¼   cup fresh lemon juice
4   tablespoons sugar
2   tablespoons unsalted butter
⅓   cup pure maple syrup
2   tablespoons Calvados

ACCOMPANIMENT:
premium-quality vanilla ice cream

Preheat broiler.

Toss apples with lemon juice and 2 tablespoons sugar. Melt butter in a shallow baking pan 6 inches from heat. Remove from oven and tilt pan back and forth to coat bottom completely with butter. Arrange apples in 1 layer in pan. Broil apples 6 inches from heat until edges are pale golden and apples are just tender, 8 to 10 minutes. Sprinkle remaining 2 tablespoons sugar over apples and broil until sugar is melted, 1 to 2 minutes.

While apples are broiling, boil maple syrup and Calvados 2 minutes.

Serve apples and ice cream topped with sauce.

Photo opposite

NECTARINES, PLUMS, AND BLUEBERRIES IN LEMONY GINGER ANISE SYRUP

Serves 4

1	lemon
½	cup water
3	(⅓-inch-thick) slices peeled fresh ginger
4	whole star anise* or ⅛ cup star anise pieces*
½	cup sugar
3	firm-ripe nectarines (¾ lb), halved, pitted, and cut into wedges
9	assorted plums (1½ lb), halved and pitted
1	cup blueberries

available at Asian markets and specialty foods shops

Remove three 3- by ½-inch pieces zest from lemon and squeeze enough juice to measure 1½ teaspoons. Simmer water with zest, 1 teaspoon lemon juice, ginger, star anise, and sugar in a saucepan, stirring, until sugar is dissolved. Cool syrup and discard star anise.

Toss together fruit, syrup, and remaining ½ teaspoon lemon juice in a bowl.

Photo opposite

CHOCOLATE-CHUNK COOKIES WITH PECANS, DRIED APRICOTS, AND TART CHERRIES

Makes about 34 cookies

2½	cups all-purpose flour
1	teaspoon baking soda
½	teaspoon baking powder
1	teaspoon salt
2	sticks (1 cup) unsalted butter, softened
1	cup granulated sugar
½	cup light brown sugar
2	large eggs
9	oz fine-quality bittersweet (not unsweetened) or semisweet chocolate, chopped into ½-inch pieces
¾	cup quartered dried apricots (4½ oz)
1	cup dried tart cherries (5 oz)
1	cup coarsely chopped pecans (4 oz)

Preheat oven to 375°F.

Whisk together flour, baking soda, baking powder, and salt in a bowl. Beat together butter and sugars in another bowl with an electric mixer until light and fluffy. Add eggs 1 at a time, beating well after each addition, and beat in flour mixture until just combined.

Stir chocolate pieces into batter with apricots, cherries, and pecans. Working in batches, drop dough by heaping tablespoons about 2 inches apart onto ungreased baking sheets and bake in upper and lower thirds of oven, switching position of sheets halfway through baking, about 12 minutes total, or until golden. Cool cookies on baking sheets on racks 5 minutes and transfer with a spatula to racks to cool.

Photo opposite

INDIVIDUAL BLUEBERRY-COCONUT POUND CAKES

Serves 4 to 6

For a more formal look, purée some blueberries with a little sugar and serve the sauce over the cakes.

1   stick (½ cup) unsalted butter, softened
¾   cup sugar
2   teaspoons freshly grated lime zest
2   large eggs
5   tablespoons heavy cream
1   cup all-purpose flour
¼   teaspoon salt
½   cup plus 3 tablespoons sweetened
     flaked coconut
½   cup blueberries

Preheat oven to 350°F and butter and flour 9 (½-cup) muffin cups (just butter if nonstick).

Beat together butter, sugar, and zest until light and fluffy. Beat in eggs, 1 at a time. Beat in cream, then flour and salt, on low speed until just combined. Stir in ½ cup coconut and gently stir in blueberries.

Spoon batter into cups and smooth tops. Sprinkle tops with remaining 3 tablespoons coconut.

Bake in middle of oven until a tester comes out clean and edges are golden brown, about 25 minutes. Invert onto a rack and cool.

KIWIFRUIT SHORTBREAD TARTS

Serves 2

For shortbread crusts
2   tablespoons sugar
½   cup all-purpose flour
½   stick (¼ cup) cold unsalted butter,
     cut into small pieces

For lime cream
½   cup sour cream
2   tablespoons sugar
1   teaspoon fresh lime juice

2   firm-ripe kiwifruits, peeled and cut
     crosswise into ¾-inch-thick slices

Preheat oven to 375°F.

Make crusts:
Pulse together sugar and flour in a food processor. Add butter, pulsing until mixture forms a crumbly dough, about 15 seconds. Divide dough in half and roll out each half between 2 sheets of wax paper into a 5½-inch round (about ¼ inch thick). Remove top sheets of wax paper and trim rounds to make perfect circles. Invert rounds onto an ungreased baking sheet and remove remaining sheets of wax paper. Bake in middle of oven until pale golden, about 8 minutes. Cool shortbread on sheet on a rack 5 minutes and transfer to rack to cool completely.

Make lime cream:
Stir together sour cream, sugar, and lime juice. Spread cream onto shortbread and top decoratively with fruit slices.

Photo opposite, top

CHOCOLATE-ORANGE TURNOVERS

Makes 4 turnovers, serving 2

1½   oz fine-quality bittersweet chocolate
     (not unsweetened), chopped
½   teaspoon freshly grated orange zest
1   puff pastry sheet (from a 17¼-oz package
     frozen puff pastry sheets), thawed
1   large egg, lightly beaten
2   teaspoons sugar

Preheat oven to 425°F and lightly butter a baking sheet.

Stir together chocolate and zest in a small bowl. Trim any uneven edges from pastry sheet and cut into 4 squares. Brush edges of squares with some egg. Put one fourth chocolate mixture on center of each square and fold each diagonally in half, forming triangles. Seal edges by gently pressing together and crimp decoratively.

Brush tops of turnovers with egg and sprinkle with sugar. Cut a small steam vent in top of each turnover. Bake on baking sheet in middle of oven until golden, about 12 minutes. Cool turnovers slightly on a rack and serve warm.

Photo left, bottom

LEMON CURD

Makes about 1⅔ cups

Serve this tangy treat with biscuits or store-bought angel food cake.

3   lemons
¾   cup sugar
2   large eggs
1   stick (½ cup) unsalted butter, cut into 4 pieces

Finely grate enough zest from lemons to measure 2 teaspoons and squeeze enough juice to measure ½ cup. Whisk together zest, juice, sugar, and eggs in a metal bowl and add butter. Set bowl over a saucepan of simmering water and cook mixture, whisking occasionally, until thickened and smooth, about 20 minutes. Serve warm or chilled.

ORANGE-VANILLA COUPE

Serves 6
Makes about 1 quart orange sorbet

In France, the term "coupe" is used to describe fancy sundaes. Our coupe—inspired by the classic American childhood favorite, the Creamsicle® bar—is hardly fancy, but its taste is sublime.

For orange sorbet
3   cups fresh orange juice
½   cup sugar (preferably superfine)

1   pint vanilla ice cream

Special equipment:
an ice-cream maker

Make orange sorbet:
Stir together orange juice and sugar until sugar is dissolved and freeze in ice-cream maker until firm enough to serve, 20 to 25 minutes.

Serve scoops of sorbet with scoops of vanilla ice cream.

GREEN-APPLE SORBET

Makes about 1¼ quarts

Gina DePalma, pastry chef at Babbo Restaurant in New York City, recently taught us a great trick: A vitamin C tablet will stop apple juice from oxidizing and turning brown. As you'll see, it's not necessary to peel or seed the apples, as all fiber will be separated out in the juicer.

⅔   cup sugar
⅓   cup water
1   (1000 mg) tablet vitamin C
6   Granny Smith apples (2⅔ lb total), cut into 1-inch wedges

Special equipment:
an electric juice extractor and an ice-cream maker

Simmer sugar and water in a small heavy saucepan, stirring until sugar is dissolved, and remove from heat.

Crush vitamin C tablet to a powder in a mortar and pestle or with the back of a spoon and place in a 1-quart container that will fit under spout of juicer. Juice apples in vegetable juicer into container and spoon off foam. Stir in sugar syrup.

Freeze sorbet in ice-cream maker until firm enough to serve, 20 to 25 minutes.

Each (¾-cup) serving about 167 calories and less than 1 gram fat

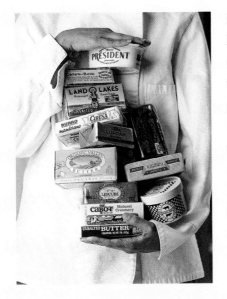

Recently, pounds and pounds of butter were softened, melted, and creamed in our kitchens during the testing of dozens of cookie and pastry recipes and one thing became extremely clear: You want to buy the best. We tasted more than 20 different brands of unsalted butter, all bought in New York City supermarkets and specialty foods shops. (Salt is used as a preservative and may mask staleness.) The results astonished us.

Most surprising? The way butter is wrapped may actually turn out to be more important than how it is made or shipped. Our three favorites were all wrapped in foil. None of the butters that were wrapped in paper even came close.

Freshness can often be a problem. While we always check the expiration date when buying milk, few of us think to look for dates on packages of butter. They are there, but they can be difficult to find and to decipher. And if the butter has been mishandled during its complex distribution process, the date can be meaningless.

What to do? If you've never detected rancidity in the butter you buy, stick with it. If, on the other hand, it has an off taste, you might want to shop around. Our tasting was by no means exhaustive, but our three favorites were Keller's European Style (also known as Plugrá, and not to be confused with Keller's plain butter); Beurre Echiré, from France; and Land O Lakes.

—Zanne Stewart

PECAN BOURBON CARAMEL SAUCE

Makes about 1½ cups

1   cup sugar
¾   cup heavy cream
3   tablespoons bourbon
1   teaspoon fresh lemon juice
1   cup toasted chopped pecans

ACCOMPANIMENT:
fine-quality vanilla ice cream

Cook sugar over moderately low heat in a dry heavy saucepan, stirring slowly with a fork (to help sugar melt evenly), until melted and pale golden. Cook caramel, without stirring, swirling pan, until deep golden. Remove pan from heat and carefully add cream, bourbon, lemon juice, and pecans (caramel will steam and harden). Return pan to heat and simmer sauce, stirring, until caramel is dissolved, about 5 minutes. Pour sauce into a bowl and cool slightly.

Photo opposite

FUDGY CHOCOLATE SAUCE

Makes about 1¼ cups

The secret to this sauce's consistency is to simmer the chocolate—it makes the sauce fudgy.

¼   cup whole milk
¼   cup heavy cream
2   tablespoons unsalted butter, cut into pieces
2   tablespoons sugar
6   oz good-quality bittersweet chocolate (not unsweetened), finely chopped

Simmer milk, cream, butter, and sugar in a small heavy saucepan over moderate heat, whisking until smooth. Remove pan from heat and add chocolate, whisking until smooth. Simmer over moderately low heat 1 minute to slightly thicken.

STRAWBERRY BALSAMIC SAUCE

Makes about 1½ cups

This sauce is great served with pound cake, ice cream, or fresh fruit such as mangoes or figs. If you prefer, the sauce can be puréed.

3   tablespoons sugar
2   tablespoons water
1   tablespoon balsamic vinegar
1   pint strawberries, stemmed and sliced

Heat sugar, water, and vinegar over moderately low heat in a small heavy saucepan, stirring until sugar is dissolved. Toss with strawberries in a bowl and let stand 5 minutes.

MANGO-LIME COULIS

Makes about 1¼ cups

Try our coulis with other tropical fruits, sorbets, coconut ice cream, or with our kiwifruit tarts (page 184).

1   ripe mango, peeled and coarsely chopped
½   cup water
2   tablespoons sugar
1   tablespoon fresh lime juice

Purée all ingredients in a blender or food processor.

Each (5 tablespoon) serving about 58 calories and less than 1 gram fat

INDEX
of recipes

Page numbers in *italics* indicate color photographs
◐ indicates recipes that can be made in 20 minutes or less
◈ indicates leaner/lighter recipes

a

ALMONDS
    Chicken, Pan-Roasted, with Oranges,
        Rosemary and, *63*, 63
    Mussels, Roasted, with Garlic and, *16*, 17
◐ ANCHO-Chile Skirt Steak, Pan-Seared, 66
ANISE Lemony Ginger Syrup, Nectarines, Plums,
    and Blueberries in, *182*, 183
APPLE(S)
◐   Broiled, with Maple Calvados Sauce,
        180, *181*
    -Fig Salsa, Feta and Walnut Quesadillas with,
        114, *115*
◈   Green-, Sorbet, 186
◐   Peanut Butter, and Bacon Sandwiches, *106*,
        106
APRICOT(S)
◈   Bulgur with, Herbed, 151
    Dried, Chocolate-Chunk Cookies, with
        Pecans, Tart Cherries and, *182*, 183
◈   Pineapple, and Jícama Salsa, Spicy, *86*, 87
ARUGULA
    Chicken Legs, Roasted, with Vegetables and,
        14, 15
◐   Fusilli with Smoked Mozzarella and, 120
◐   Goat Cheese, and Beet Sandwiches, Warm,
        105, 105
    Salad, -Parsley, with Chickpeas, Pickles, and
        Sherry-Mustard Vinaigrette, *158*, 158
ASIAN
    Chicken and Watercress Salad, Crispy, *36*, 37
    Chile Dressing, -Style, Potato Salad
        with, 144
◐   Peanut Sauce, 89
◈   Salmon Burgers with Pickled Cucumber on
        Pumpernickel, 110, *111*
    Shrimp and Noodles, 122
◈ ASPARAGUS with Peperonata, 142
AVOCADO. *See also* Guacamole
    and Olive Quesadillas, *115*, 115

B

BACON
◐   and Cheddar on Raisin Bread, Grilled, *106*,
        106
◐   Endive, and Stilton Salad, 156, *157*
    Frisée Salad with Lardons and Poached Eggs,
        38, 39
◐◈   Mustard Dressing, Low-Fat, *162*, 164
    Orzo Risotto with Butternut Squash and, 121
◐   Peanut Butter, and Apple Sandwiches, *106*,
        106
BALSAMIC (VINEGAR)
◐   Beets and Red Onions, 145
◐   Strawberry Sauce, 189
BARLEY Vegetable Soup, 101
BASIL
    Pesto Eggplant Pizza, 131
◐◈   Salsa Verde with Tomatoes, 141
◐   Shrimp and Corn with, *28*, 29
◈   Tomato Clam Sauce, Linguine with, *118*, 119
◈ BASMATI and Cumin Pilaf, 150
◐ BASS, Sea, Seared, with Fresh Herbs and Lemon,
    62, *63*
BEAN(S). *See also* Chickpea(s); Green Bean(s)
◐◈   Black, Salsa and Turkey Tortilla Rolls, *108*,
        108
    Pasta Fagiole, 125
◐   Red, Mizuna, and Chopped Parmesan Salad,
        161
    Refried, and Hot Pepper Jack Quesadillas
        with Pickled Onion, 114, *115*
    White, Bruschetta with Walnuts and, *172*, 172
    White, Sausage, and Escarole Soup, 95
◈   White, Tomato, and Goat Cheese Pizza, 132
BEEF. *See also* Steak(s)
    burgers, forming and cooking, 112
    Cheeseburgers, Guacamole, *113*, 113
    Corned Beef Hash, 22, *23*
BEET(S)
    Borscht, *92*, 93

Goat Cheese, and Arugula Sandwiches,
Warm, *105*, 105
and Red Onions, Balsamic, 145
and Spinach Salad, Sesame, *158*, 159
BELL PEPPER(S). *See* Pepper(s); Red Pepper(s)
BERRY Compote with Crispy Won Ton Strips and
Vanilla Ice Cream, 179
BLACK-BEAN Salsa and Turkey Tortilla Rolls,
108, 108
BLUEBERRY(IES)
-Coconut Pound Cakes, Individual, 184
Nectarines, and Plums in Lemony Ginger
Anise Syrup, *182*, 183
BOK CHOY, Sesame-Spinach, with Seared
Salmon, *68*, 68
BORSCHT, *92*, 93
BOURBON Pecan Caramel Sauce, *188*, 189
BREAD CRUMB(S)
Buttered, Leeks Broiled with,
135, 137
Pasta with Capers, Garlic and,
120, 120
Toasted, Topping for Pasta, 129
BROCCOLI, Pork Stir-Fry with Ginger and,
Spicy, 70
BROCCOLI RABE
boiled, 62, 140
Pasta with Mussels, Roasted Red Peppers
and, *126*, 127
Pizza, 133
BROWN RICE, and Vegetable Salad, Crunchy,
152, *153*
BRUSCHETTA with White Beans and Walnuts,
172, 172
BULGUR, Herbed, with Apricots, 151
BURGERS
Cheeseburgers, Guacamole, *113*, 113
forming and cooking, 112
Salmon, with Pickled Cucumber on
Pumpernickel, Asian, 110, *111*
Turkey, Herbed, 113
BUTTER
Ginger, Grilled Salmon Steaks with,
80, *81*
Gremolata, Sautéed Sole with, 69
selecting for freshness, 187
BUTTERNUT SQUASH, Orzo Risotto with Bacon
and, 121

C

CABBAGE and Cucumber, Pickled, *59*, 141
CAKE(S)
Chocolate, Flourless, 179

Pound, Blueberry-Coconut, Individual, 184
CALVADOS Maple Sauce, Broiled Apples with,
180, *181*
CALZONES, Red and Yellow Bell Pepper,
133
CANTALOUPE, Watermelon, and Red Pepper
Salsa, *86*, *87*
CAPERS, Pasta with Garlic, Bread Crumbs and,
120, 120
CARAMEL Pecan Bourbon Sauce, *188*, 189
CARAWAY Rice Cakes, 151
CARROT(S)
Baby, and Haricots Verts with Mustard-Dill
Sauce, 144
Hummus, and Cucumber Lavash Wraps, 110
Moroccan Spicy, *139*, 139
Soup, and Red Lentil, *101*, 101
CAST IRON, to season, 72
CAULIFLOWER Goat Cheese Gratin, 142
CELERY Tomatillo Salsa, *86*, *87*
CHARCOAL, grilling tips, 79
CHEDDAR and Bacon on Raisin Bread, Grilled,
106, 106
CHEESE. *See also* Goat Cheese; Parmesan
Cheddar and Bacon on Raisin Bread, Grilled,
106, 106
Corn on the Cob with Lime and, *136*, 137
Feta, Shrimp, Pan-Braised, with, 71
Feta and Walnut Quesadillas with Apple-Fig
Salsa, 114, *115*
Mozzarella, Smoked, Fusilli with Arugula
and, 120
Mozzarella, Smoked, and Yellow Squash
Pizzettes, Grilled, *130*, 130
Pepper Jack, Hot, and Refried Bean
Quesadillas with Pickled Onion, 114, *115*
Pizza Margherita, 131
Stilton, Endive, and Bacon Salad, 156, *157*
Stilton Sauce, Rib-Eye Steak with, *81*, 81
Swiss, with Walnuts and Mustard, *170*, 170
CHEESEBURGERS, Guacamole, *113*, 113
CHEF'S SALAD, A New, *34*, 35
CHERRIES, Tart, Chocolate-Chunk Cookies, with
Pecans, Dried Apricots and, *182*, 183
CHERRY TOMATO and Lamb Kebabs, Grilled,
with Guacamole, 78
CHICKEN
and Chickpea Stew, Saffron, *26*, 27
Cornmeal-Crusted, with Toasted Corn Salsa,
57, 58
grilling time, 85
Legs, Roasted, with Vegetables and Arugula,
14, 15
Pan-Roasted, with Oranges, Rosemary, and
Almonds, *63*, 63

Roasted with Tomatoes, Potatoes, and Olives, 30, 31

Sandwiches, Broiled, and Roasted Pepper, 108, 109

Sandwiches, and Mango, Curried, 103, 104

Smoked, and Sugar Snap Pea Salad with Mint, 42, 43

Soup, Chinese Noodle, 93

Soup, Pozole, 98

Stir-Fry with Shiitakes, Snow Peas, and Pea Shoots, 65

and Watercress Salad, Crispy Asian, 36, 37

CHICKPEA(S)

Arugula-Parsley Salad with Pickles, Sherry-Mustard Vinaigrette and, 158, 158

and Chicken Stew, Saffron, 26, 27

Dip, Cumin, 172, 172

Dip, Garlic, Parsley and, 170, 171

Hummus, Carrot, and Cucumber Lavash Wraps, 110

CHICORY Salad with Walnuts and Goat Cheese, 161

CHILE(S). See also Chipotle

Ancho-, Skirt Steak, Pan-Seared, 66

Dressing, Asian-Style, Potato Salad with, 144

Jalapeño-Spiced Mussels, 68

Mint Chutney with Orange and, 89

Purée, Corn Soup with, Chilled, 98

CHINESE

Chicken Noodle Soup, 93

Turkey in Jade, 50, 51

CHIPOTLE

about, 107

Chutney Dressing, Low-Fat, 162, 165

Mayo, Smoked Turkey, and Mango Wraps, 107

Tomato, Charred, and Mango Salsa, 88, 88

Yogurt Sauce with Cumin, 89

CHOCOLATE

Cake, Flourless, 179

Cookies, -Chunk, with Pecans, Dried Apricots, and Tart Cherries, 182, 183

Sauce, Fudgy, 189

Turnovers, -Orange, 185, 185

CHOWDER, Crab, 94, 94

CHUTNEY

Dressing, Chipotle, Low-Fat, 162, 165

Dressing, Garlic, 165, 165

Mint, with Orange and Chile, 89

CILANTRO

Jícama Sticks with Lime and, 174

-Parsley Sauce, Steamed Clams with, 66, 67

Thai Ground-Pork Salad with Mint and, 48, 49

CLAM(S)

Dip, Creamy, 170, 171

Sauce, Tomato Basil, Linguine with, 118, 119

Steamed, with Cilantro-Parsley Sauce, 66, 67

COCONUT MILK and Shrimp Soup with Asian Noodles, 100

COD, Fried, Tacos, 70

COFFEE Soufflés with Mocha Sauce, 177, 178

COLLARD GREENS, Spicy, 145

COMPOTE, Berry, with Crispy Won Ton Strips and Vanilla Ice Cream, 179

COOKIES, Chocolate-Chunk, with Pecans, Dried Apricots, and Tart Cherries, 182, 183

CORIANDER-Cumin Spice Rub, Pork Chops with, 64, 65

CORN

on the Cob with Cheese and Lime, 136, 137

Frittata, Scallion, Potato and, 73

and Shrimp with Basil, 28, 29

Soup with Chile Purée, Chilled, 98

Succotash, 138

Toasted, Salsa, Cornmeal-Crusted Chicken with, 57, 58

CORNED BEEF Hash, 22, 23

CORNMEAL-Crusted Chicken with Toasted Corn Salsa, 57, 58

COUSCOUS

Pea and Mint, Seared Sesame Scallops with, 71, 71

and Sugar Snap Pea Salad with Pistachios, 128

Vegetable, 75

CRAB

Canapés on Cumin Pita Toasts, Light, 174

Chowder, 94, 94

Melt Sandwiches, 104, 105

CRANBERRY Sauce, Savory Dried, 88, 88

CUCUMBER

Hummus, and Carrot Lavash Wraps, 110

Pickled, and Cabbage, 59, 141

Pickled, Salmon Burgers with, on Pumpernickel, 110, 111

Sesame, and Watercress Salad, 156

CUMIN

and Basmati Pilaf, 150

Chickpea Dip, 172, 172

Chipotle Yogurt Sauce with, 89

Pita Toasts, Crab Canapés on, Light, 174

Spice Rub, -Coriander, Pork Chops with, 64, 65

CURRY(IED)

Chicken and Mango Sandwiches, 103, 104

Oil, Rib-Eye Steaks, Grilled, on Sautéed
Onions and Garlic Croûtes with, *18*, 19
Peas with Cilantro, 141
Salmon, Pan-Roasted, with Ginger and,
58, *59*

D

DANDELION Salad with Warm Hazelnut
Vinaigrette, *155*, 156
DATES, Mustard Greens with Citrus Juice and,
159
DESSERT SAUCE(S)
Fudgy Chocolate, 189
Maple Calvados, Broiled Apples with,
180, *181*
Mocha, *178*, 178
Mocha, Coffee Soufflés with, *177*, 178
Pecan Bourbon Caramel, *188*, 189
Strawberry Balsamic, 189
DILL-Mustard Sauce, Baby Carrots and Haricots
Verts with, 144
DIPS AND SPREADS
Chickpea, Garlic, and Parsley, *170*, 171
Clam, Creamy, *170*, 171
Crab Canapés, Light, on Cumin Pita Toasts,
174
Lemon-Yogurt, Caramelized Figs with, 180
Red Pepper, with Walnuts, *170*, 171
Sun-Dried Tomato and Roasted Red Pepper,
174, 174
Swiss Cheese with Walnuts and Mustard, *170*,
170
White Beans and Walnuts, Bruschetta with,
172, 172

e

EGG(S)
Corned Beef Hash, 22, 23
Frittata, Corn, Scallion, and Potato, 73
Frittata, Smoked Salmon, with Goat Cheese,
74, 74
Poached, Frisée Salad with Lardons and, *38*,
39
Salmon Kedgeree, 24, 25
Soufflés, Coffee, with Mocha Sauce,
177, 178
EGGPLANT
Broiled, Spicy Soba Noodles with, 122
Pizza, Pesto, 131
ENDIVE, Stilton, and Bacon Salad, 156, *157*
ESCAROLE, White Bean, and Sausage Soup, 95

F

FENNEL
Italian Sausage, Sweet, with Onion and, 75
Pita Toasts, 173
and Shrimp Risotto, *20*, 21
FETA
Shrimp, Pan-Braised, with, 71
and Walnut Quesadillas with Apple-Fig Salsa,
114, *115*
FETTUCCINE with Pumpkin Seed Pesto, 121
FIG(S)
-Apple Salsa, Feta and Walnut Quesadillas
with, 114, *115*
Caramelized, with Lemon-Yogurt Dip, 180
FILET MIGNON with Mustard Sauce, *62*, 62
FISH *See also* Salmon; Tuna
Cod, Fried, Tacos, 70
grilling time, 85
Halibut, Pan-Seared, with Salsa Verde, 60, *61*
Red Snapper, Grilled Indian-Spiced Whole,
with Mango Raita, 80
Sea Bass, Seared, with Fresh Herbs and
Lemon, *62*, 63
Sole, Sautéed, with Gremolata Butter, 69
FRISÉE Salad with Lardons and Poached Eggs,
38, 39
FRITTATA
Corn, Scallion, and Potato, 73
Smoked Salmon, with Goat Cheese, 74, 74
FRUIT. *See* names of fruits
FUSILLI with Arugula and Smoked Mozzarella,
120

G

GARLIC
Chickpea, and Parsley Dip, *170*, 171
Chutney Dressing, *165*, 165
Croûtes, Grilled Rib-Eye Steaks on Sautéed
Onions and, with Curry Oil, *18*, 19
Green Noodles with, 123
Gremolata Butter, Sautéed Sole with, 69
Lamb Chops, Lemon-, with Yogurt Sauce, 74
Mussels, Roasted, with Almonds and,
16, 17
Pasta with Capers, Bread Crumbs and, *120*,
120
Tortellini with Baby Spinach and, 123
GAZPACHO, Quick, with Parsley Pesto, 100
GINGER
Butter, Salmon Steaks, Grilled, with, 80, *81*
-Miso Vinaigrette, 166

Pork Stir-Fry with Broccoli and, Spicy, 70

Salmon, Pan-Roasted, with Curry and,
58, 59

Syrup, Lemony Anise, Nectarines, Plums,
and Blueberries in, 182, 183

GOAT CHEESE

Beet, and Arugula Sandwiches, Warm, 105,
105

Cauliflower Gratin, 142

Chicory Salad with Walnuts and, 161

Smoked Salmon Frittata with,
74, 74

White Bean, and Tomato Pizza, 132

GRAINS. See also names of grains
cooking and handling, 149

GREEK SALAD with Tuna, 40, 41

GREEN BEAN(S)

Asian Pear, and Radicchio Salad, 161

Haricots Verts and Baby Carrots with
Mustard-Dill Sauce, 144

with Pecan Pesto, 144

GRILLING

charcoal, 79

chart (indoor/outdoor), 84-85

stove-top pans, 82

GRITS Triangles, Fried, 152

GUACAMOLE

Cheeseburgers, 113, 113

Dressing, 166

Lamb and Cherry Tomato Kebabs, Grilled,
with, 78

H

HALIBUT, Pan-Seared, with Salsa Verde,
60, 61

HARICOTS VERTS and Baby Carrots with
Mustard-Dill Sauce, 144

HASH, Corned Beef, 22, 23

HAZELNUT Vinaigrette, Warm, Dandelion Salad
with, 155, 156

HERBS. See names of herbs

HORS D'OEUVRES. See Snacks and Hors
d'Oeuvres

HUMMUS

Carrot, and Cucumber Lavash Wraps, 110

Chickpea Cumin Dip, 172

Chickpea, Garlic, and Parsley Dip, 171

I

INDIAN-Spiced, Whole Red Snapper with Mango
Raita, Grilled, 80

ITALIAN SAUSAGE, Sweet, with Fennel and
Onion, 75

J

JALAPEÑO-Spiced Mussels, 68

JASMINE RICE, Herbed, 147, 148

JÍCAMA

Pineapple, and Apricot Salsa, Spicy,
86, 87

Sticks with Cilantro and Lime, 174

K

KEBABS, Lamb and Cherry Tomato, Grilled, with
Guacamole, 78

KIWIFRUIT Shortbread Tarts, 184, 185

L

LAMB

Chops, Lemon-Garlic, with Yogurt
Sauce, 74

Kebabs, and Cherry Tomato, Grilled, with
Guacamole, 78

LEEK(S)

Broiled with Buttered Bread Crumbs,
135, 137

and Mushroom Soup, 91, 93

LEMON

Curd, 186

Gremolata Butter, Sautéed Sole with, 69

Lamb Chops, -Garlic, with Yogurt
Sauce, 74

Sea Bass, Seared, with Fresh Herbs and, 62,
63

Syrup, Ginger Anise, Nectarines, Plums, and
Blueberries in, 182, 183

Tomatillo Sauce, Campanelle with, 124

-Yogurt Dip, Caramelized Figs with,
180

LENTIL

Soup, Red, and Carrot, 101, 101

Soup with Spinach and Tomato, 95

LIME

Corn on the Cob with Cheese and,
136, 137

Jícama Sticks with Cilantro and, 174

-Mango Coulis, 189

Salt, Sweet Potato Chips with, 169, 170

LINGUINE with Tomato-Basil Clam Sauce,
118, 119

m

MANGO
  and Chicken Sandwiches, Curried, *103*, 104
  Coulis, -Lime, 189
  Raita, Red Snapper, Grilled Indian-Spiced
    Whole, with, 80
  Salsa, Charred Tomato, Chipotle and,
    88, *88*
  Turkey, Smoked, and Chipotle Mayo Wraps,
    107
MAPLE Calvados Sauce, Broiled Apples with,
  180, *181*
MARINARA SAUCE, Orecchiette with Turkey
  Sausage and, 128
MARSALA, Veal Scallopini with Mushrooms
  and, 73
MINT
  Chutney with Orange and Chile, 89
  Couscous, Pea and, Seared Sesame Scallops
    with, *71*, 71
  Smoked Chicken and Sugar Snap Pea Salad
    with, *42*, 43
  Thai Ground-Pork Salad with Cilantro and,
    48, 49
MISO
  -Ginger Vinaigrette, 166
  Soup, 97
MIZUNA, Chopped Parmesan, and Red Bean
  Salad, 161
MOCHA
  Sauce, *177*, 178
  Sauce, Coffee Soufflés with, *177*, 178
MOROCCAN Spicy Carrots, *139*, 139
MOZZARELLA
  Pizza Margherita, 131
  Smoked, Fusilli with Arugula and, 120
  Smoked, and Yellow Squash Pizzettes,
    Grilled, *130*, 130
MULLIGATAWNY Soup, Pumpkin, 97
MUSHROOM(S)
  Portabella, Grilled, with Herbed Sour
    Cream, 83
  Shiitakes, Chicken Stir-Fry with Snow Peas,
    Pea Shoots and, 65
  Soup, and Leek, *91*, 93
  Veal Scallopini with Marsala and, 73
MUSSELS
  Jalapeño-Spiced, 68
  Pasta with Roasted Red Peppers, Broccoli
    Rabe and, *126*, 127
  Roasted, with Almonds and Garlic, *16*, 17
MUSTARD
  Dressing, Bacon, Low-Fat, *162*, 164
  Sauce, -Dill, Baby Carrots and Haricots Verts
    with, 144
  Sauce, Filet Mignon with, *62*, 62
  Sauce, Sea Scallops, Sautéed, with, 60, *61*
  Swiss Cheese with Walnuts and, *170*, 170
  Vinaigrette, Sherry-, Arugula-Parsley Salad
    with Chickpeas, Pickles, and, *158*, 158
MUSTARD GREENS with Citrus Juice and
  Dates, 159

n

NECTARINES, Plums, and Blueberries in Lemony
  Ginger Anise Syrup, *182*, 183
NONSTICK SKILLETS, care of, 61
NOODLE(S)
  Asian, Spicy Shrimp and Coconut Milk Soup
    with, 100
  Green, with Garlic, 123
  and Shrimp, Asian, 122
  Soba, Spicy, with Broiled Eggplant, 122
  Soup, Chinese Chicken, 93
NUT(S). *See* names of nuts

o

OLIVE(S)
  and Avocado Quesadillas, *115*, 115
  Chicken Roasted with Tomatoes, Potatoes
    and, *30*, 31
  Gemelli with Olivada and Roasted Red
    Peppers, 124
  Relish, -Oregano, Grilled Strip Steaks with,
    77, *78*
ONION(S)
  to chop, 160
  Italian Sausage, Sweet, with Fennel and, 75
  Pickled, 114
  Pickled, Refried Bean and Hot Pepper Jack
    Quesadillas with, 114, *115*
  Red, and Beets, Balsamic, 145
  Sautéed, Grilled Rib-Eye Steaks on Garlic
    Croûtes and, with Curry Oil, *18*, 19
ORANGE(S)
  Chicken, Pan-Roasted, with Rosemary,
    Almonds and, *63*, 63
  -Chocolate Turnovers, *185*, 185
  Mint Chutney with Chile and, 89
  -Vanilla Coupe, 186
OREGANO-Olive Relish, Grilled Strip Steaks
  with, 77, *78*
ORZO Risotto with Bacon and Butternut Squash,
  121

P

PARMESAN
  Chopped, Mizuna, and Red Bean Salad, 161
  Polenta, Creamy, 64, 153
  Popcorn with, Spicy, 173
PARSLEY
  -Arugula Salad with Chickpeas, Pickles, and
    Sherry-Mustard Vinaigrette, 158, 158
  Chickpea, and Garlic Dip, 170, 171
  -Cilantro Sauce, Steamed Clams with, 66, 67
  Gremolata Butter, Sautéed Sole with, 69
  Pesto, Gazpacho with, Quick, 100
  Salsa Verde with Tomatoes, 141
PARSNIP Shoestring Crisps, 173
PASTA. See also Noodle(s)
  Bread-Crumb Topping, Toasted, for, 129
  Campanelle with Lemon Tomatillo Sauce, 124
  with Capers, Garlic, and Bread Crumbs, 120,
    120
  cooking guidelines, 125
  Fagiole, 125
  Fettuccine with Pumpkin Seed Pesto, 121
  Fusilli with Arugula and Smoked Mozzarella,
    120
  Gemelli with Olivada and Roasted Red
    Peppers, 124
  Linguine with Tomato-Basil Clam Sauce, 118,
    119
  Malfada with Smoked Salmon and Sugar
    Snap Peas, 124
  with Mussels, Roasted Red Peppers, and
    Broccoli Rabe, 126, 127
  Orecchiette with Turkey Sausage and
    Marinara Sauce, 128
  Orzo Risotto with Bacon and Butternut
    Squash, 121
  "Rags" with a Thousand Herbs, 117, 119
  Salad, Warm, with Baby Spinach and Tuna,
    54, 55
  Spaghetti with Ramps, 129, 129
  Tortellini with Baby Spinach and Garlic, 123
PEA(S). See also Sugar Snap Pea(s)
  Couscous, and Mint, Seared Sesame Scallops
    with, 71, 71
  Curried, with Cilantro, 141
  Shoots, Chicken Stir-Fry with Shiitakes,
    Snow Peas and, 65
  Snow Peas, Chicken Stir-Fry with Shiitakes,
    Pea Shoots and, 65
  Soup with Tarragon, Chilled, 97
PEANUT BUTTER, Apple, and Bacon Sandwiches,
    106, 106
PEANUT SAUCE, Asian, 89

PEAR, Asian, Green Bean, and Radicchio Salad,
    161
PECAN(S)
  Bourbon Caramel Sauce, 188, 189
  Chocolate-Chunk Cookies, with Dried
    Apricots, Tart Cherries and, 182, 183
  Pesto, Green Beans with, 144
PEPPER JACK, Hot, and Refried Bean Quesadillas
    with Pickled Onion, 114, 115
PEPPER(S). See also Chile(s); Red Pepper(s)
  Asparagus with Peperonata, 142
  Calzones, Yellow and Red, 133
  Pickle-, Vinaigrette, Grilled Steak Salad
    with, 44, 45
  to quick roast and peel, 127
  Roasted, and Broiled Chicken Sandwiches,
    108, 109
PESTO
  Eggplant Pizza, 131
  Parsley, Gazpacho with, Quick, 100
  Pecan, Green Beans with, 144
  Pumpkin Seed, Fettuccine with, 121
PICKLE(S), PICKLED
  Arugula-Parsley Salad with Chickpeas,
    Sherry-Mustard Vinaigrette and,
    158, 158
  Cucumber, Salmon Burgers with, on
    Pumpernickel, 110, 111
  Cucumber and Cabbage, 59, 141
  Onion, 114
  Onion, Refried Bean and Hot Pepper Jack
    Quesadillas with, 114, 115
  -Pepper Vinaigrette, Grilled Steak Salad
    with, 44, 45
PILAF, Basmati and Cumin, 150
PINEAPPLE, Apricot, and Jícama Salsa, Spicy,
    86, 87
PISTACHIOS, Couscous and Sugar Snap Pea Salad
    with, 128
PITA TOASTS
  Cumin, Crab Canapés on, Light, 174
  Fennel, 173
PIZZA
  Broccoli Rabe, 133
  Margherita, 131
  Pesto Eggplant, 131
  White Bean, Tomato, and Goat
    Cheese, 132
PIZZETTES,
  Smoked Mozzarella and Yellow Squash,
    Grilled, 130, 130
PLANTAIN Soup, 94, 95
PLUMS, Nectarines, and Blueberries in Lemony
    Ginger Anise Syrup, 182, 183
POLENTA, Creamy Parmesan, 64, 153

POPCORN with Parmesan, Spicy, 173
PORK. *See also* Bacon; Sausage
  Chops with Coriander-Cumin Spice Rub,
    64, 65
  grilling time, 84
  Stir-Fry with Broccoli and Ginger,
    Spicy, 70
  Thai Ground-, Salad with Mint and Cilantro,
    48, 49
PORTABELLA MUSHROOMS, Grilled, with
  Herbed Sour Cream, 83
POTATO(ES)
  Chicken Roasted with Tomatoes, Olives and,
    30, 31
  Frittata, Corn, Scallion and, 73
  Galettes, Crisp, *62*, 140
  Mashed, 143
  mashing, equipment for, 143
  Salad with Asian-Style Chile
    Dressing, 144
  Salad, Herbed, 138, *139*
POUND CAKES, Blueberry-Coconut, Individual,
  184
POZOLE Chicken Soup, 98
PROCEDURES. *See also* Grilling
  burgers, forming and cooking, 112
  cast iron, to season, 72
  nonstick skillets, care of, 61
  onions, to chop, 160
  pasta, cooking guidelines, 125
  peeling, equipment for, 140
  peppers, to quick roast and peel, 127
  potato mashing, equipment for, 14
  puréeing, equipment for, 99
  rice and grains, cooking and handling, 149
  soups, to quickly chill, 96
PUMPKIN Mulligatawny Soup, 97
PUMPKIN SEED(S)
  Pesto, Fettuccine with, 121
  Toasted Spiced, 173
PURÉE
  Chile, Corn Soup with, Chilled, 98
  equipment for, 99

Q

QUESADILLAS
  Feta and Walnut, with Apple-Fig Salsa, 114,
    115
  Olive and Avocado, Ripe, *115*, 115
  Refried Bean, and Hot Pepper Jack, with
    Pickled Onion, 114, *115*
QUINOA with Tarragon and Sugar Snap
  Peas, 148

r

RADICCHIO, Green Bean, and Asian Pear Salad,
  161
RADISH SPROUTS, Tuna Steaks, Seared, with Soy
  Broth and, 69
RAITA, Mango, Red Snapper, Grilled Indian-
  Spiced Whole, with, 80
RAMPS, Spaghetti with, *129*, 129
RANCH DRESSING, Herbed, Low-Fat, *162*, 164
RED ONIONS and Beets, Balsamic, 145
RED PEPPER(S). *See also* Pepper(s)
  Dip, with Walnuts, *170*, 171
  Roasted, Gemelli with Olivada and, 124
  Roasted, Pasta with Mussels, Broccoli Rabe
    and, *126*, 127
  Watermelon, and Cantaloupe Salsa, *86*, 87
  and Yellow Bell Pepper Calzones, 133
RED SNAPPER, Grilled Indian-Spiced Whole,
  with Mango Raita, 80
REFRIED BEAN and Hot Pepper Jack Quesadillas
  with Pickled Onion, 114, *115*
RELISH, Olive-Oregano, Grilled Strip Steaks
  with, *77*, 78
RIB-EYE STEAK(S)
  Grilled, on Sautéed Onions and Garlic
    Croûtes with Curry Oil, *18, 19*
  with Stilton Sauce, *81*, 81
RICE
  Basmati and Cumin Pilaf, 150
  Brown, and Vegetable Salad, Crunchy, 152,
    153
  Cakes, Caraway, 151
  cooking and handling, 149
  Foolproof Long-Grain, 153
  Jasmine, Herbed, *147*, 148
  Risotto Milanese, *150*, 150
  Risotto, Shrimp and Fennel, *20, 21*
  Salmon Kedgeree, *24, 25*
RISOTTO
  Milanese, *150*, 150
  Orzo, with Bacon and Butternut Squash, 121
  Shrimp and Fennel, *20, 21*
ROSEMARY, Chicken, Pan-Roasted, with
  Oranges, Almonds and, *63*, 63

s

SAFFRON Chicken and Chickpea Stew, *26, 27*
SALAD(S)
  Arugula-Parsley, with Chickpeas, Pickles,
    and Sherry-Mustard Vinaigrette, *158*, 158
  Chef's, A New, *34, 35*

Chicken, Smoked, and Sugar Snap Pea, with
  Mint, *42, 43*
Chicken and Watercress, Crispy Asian,
  36, 37
Chicory, with Walnuts and Goat Cheese, 161
Chopped, Low-Fat, 159
Couscous and Sugar Snap Pea with
  Pistachios, 128
Dandelion, with Warm Hazelnut Vinaigrette,
  155, 156
Endive, Stilton, and Bacon, 156, *157*
Everyday, 163
Frisée, with Lardons and Poached Eggs, *38,
  39*
Greek, with Tuna, *40, 41*
Green Bean, Asian Pear, and Radicchio, 161
mix-ins for, 167
Mizuna, Chopped Parmesan, and Red Bean,
  161
Mustard Greens with Citrus Juice and Dates,
  159
Pasta, Warm, with Baby Spinach and Tuna,
  54, 55
Potato, with Asian-Style Chile Dressing, 144
Potato, Herbed, 138, *139*
Sesame, Cucumber, and Watercress, 156
Shrimp Cocktail Exotique, *46, 47*
Steak, Grilled, with Pickle-Pepper
  Vinaigrette, *44, 45*
Thai Ground-Pork, with Mint and Cilantro,
  48, 49
Tuna "Chop Chop," Stir-Fried, *52, 53*
Turkey in Jade, Chinese, *50, 51*
Vegetable and Brown Rice, Crunchy,
  152, 153
SALAD DRESSING. *See also* Vinaigrette
Bacon Mustard, Low-Fat, *162, 164*
Chile, Asian-Style, Potato Salad with, 144
Chipotle Chutney, Low-Fat, *162, 165*
Chutney Garlic, *165, 165*
Guacamole, 166
Ranch, Herbed, Low-Fat, *162, 164*
Thousand Island, Low-Fat, *162, 163*
SALMON
Burgers with Pickled Cucumber on
  Pumpernickel, Asian, 110, *111*
Kedgeree, *24, 25*
Pan-Roasted, with Ginger and Curry,
  58, 59
Seared, with Sesame-Spinach Bok Choy,
  68, 68
Smoked, Frittata with Goat Cheese, *74, 74*
Smoked, Malfada with Sugar Snap Peas and,
  124
Steaks, Grilled, with Ginger Butter, 80, *81*

SALSA
Apple-Fig, Feta and Walnut Quesadillas
  with, 114, *115*
Black-Bean, and Turkey Tortilla Rolls, *108,*
  108
Corn, Toasted, Cornmeal-Crusted Chicken
  with, *57, 58*
Pineapple, Apricot, and Jícama, Spicy, *86, 87*
Tomatillo Celery, *86, 87*
Tomato, Charred, Chipotle, and Mango, 88,
  88
Verde, Pan-Seared Halibut with, *60, 61*
Verde, Tomatoes with, 141
Watermelon, Cantaloupe, and Red Pepper,
  86, 87
SANDWICHES. *See also* Burgers; Quesadillas;
  Wraps
Cheddar and Bacon on Raisin Bread,
  Grilled, *106,* 106
Chicken, Broiled, and Roasted Pepper,
  108, 109
Chicken and Mango, Curried, *103,* 104
Crab Melt, 104, *105*
Goat Cheese, Beet, and Arugula, Warm, *105,*
  105
Peanut Butter, Apple, and Bacon, *106,* 106
Tortilla Rolls, Turkey and Black-Bean Salsa,
  108, 108
Turkey-Watercress Club, *109, 109*
SAUCE(S). *See also* Dessert Sauce(s); Pesto; Salsa
Chipotle Yogurt, with Cumin, 89
Cilantro-Parsley, Clams, Steamed, with, 66,
  67
Cranberry, Savory Dried, *88,* 88
Lemon Tomatillo, Campanelle with, 124
Mustard-Dill, Carrots, Baby, and Haricots
  Verts with, 144
Mustard, Filet Mignon with, *62, 62*
Mustard, Sea Scallops, Sautéed, with,
  60, *61*
Peanut, Asian, 89
Stilton, Rib-Eye Steak with, *81, 81*
Tomato-Basil Clam, Linguine with, *118, 119*
Yogurt, Lamb Chops, Lemon-Garlic, with,
  74
SAUSAGE
Sweet Italian, with Fennel and Onion, 75
Turkey, Orecchiette with Marinara Sauce
  and, 128
White Bean, and Escarole Soup, 95
SCALLION, Corn, and Potato, Frittata, 73
SCALLOPS
Sea, Sautéed, with Mustard Sauce, 60, *61*
Sesame, Seared, with Pea and Mint
  Couscous, *71, 71*
SEA BASS, Seared, with Fresh Herbs and Lemon,
  62, 63

SESAME
   Cucumber, and Watercress Salad, 156
   Scallops, Seared, with Pea and Mint
     Couscous, 71, 71
   -Soy Sweet Potatoes, 138
   -Soy Vinaigrette, 166
   Spinach and Beet Salad, 158, 159
   -Spinach Bok Choy with Seared Salmon, 68,
     68
SHELLFISH. See Clam(s); Crab; Mussels; Scallops;
     Shrimp
SHIITAKES, Chicken Stir-Fry with Snow Peas, Pea
     Shoots and, 65
SHORTBREAD Tarts, Kiwifruit, 184, 185
SHRIMP
   Cocktail Exotique, 46, 47
   and Coconut Milk Soup with Asian Noodles,
     100
   and Corn with Basil, 28, 29
   and Fennel Risotto, 20, 21
   grilling time, 85
   and Noodles, Asian, 122
   Pan-Braised, with Feta, 71
SKIRT STEAK, Ancho-Chile, Pan-Seared, 66
SMOKED SALMON
   Frittata with Goat Cheese, 74, 74
   Malfada with Sugar Snap Peas and, 124
SNACKS AND HORS D'OEUVRES. See also Dips
     and Spreads; Toasts
   Jícama Sticks with Cilantro and Lime, 174
   pantry staples, 175
   Parsnip Shoestring Crisps, 173
   Popcorn with Parmesan, Spicy, 173
   Pumpkin Seeds, Toasted Spiced, 173
   Sweet-Potato Chips with Lime Salt, 169, 170
SNOW PEAS, Chicken Stir-Fry with Shiitakes, Pea
     Shoots and, 65
SOBA NOODLES, Spicy, with Broiled Eggplant,
     122
SOLE, Sautéed, with Gremolata Butter, 69
SORBET
   Green-Apple, 186
   Orange-Vanilla Coupe, 186
SOUFFLÉS, Coffee, with Mocha Sauce, 177, 178
SOUP
   Barley Vegetable, 101
   Borscht, 92, 93
   Chicken Noodle, Chinese, 93
   Chicken Pozole, 98
   to chill, quickly, 96
   Corn, with Chile Purée, Chilled, 98
   Crab Chowder, 94, 94
   Gazpacho, Quick, with Parsley Pesto, 100
   Lentil, with Spinach and Tomato, 95
   Miso, 97

   Mushroom and Leek, 91, 93
   Pea, with Tarragon, Chilled, 97
   Plantain, 94, 95
   Pumpkin Mulligatawny, 97
   puréeing, equipment for, 99
   Shrimp and Coconut Milk, with Asian
     Noodles, 100
   White Bean, Sausage, and Escarole, 95
   Zucchini Herb, Chilled, 96
SOUR CREAM, Herbed, Grilled Portabella
     Mushrooms with, 83
SOY
   Broth, Tuna Steaks, Seared with Radish
     Sprouts and, 69
   -Sesame Sweet Potatoes, 138
   -Sesame Vinaigrette, 166
SPAGHETTI with Ramps, 129, 129
SPICE RUB
   Coriander-Cumin, Pork Chops with, 64, 65
   Indian, Red Snapper, Grilled Whole, with
     Mango Raita, 80
SPINACH
   Baby, Pasta Salad, Warm, with Tuna and, 54,
     55
   Baby, Tortellini with Garlic and, 123
   Lentil Soup with Tomato and, 95
   Salad, and Beet, Sesame, 158, 159
   Sesame-, Bok Choy with Seared Salmon, 68,
     68
SPROUTS, Radish, Tuna Steaks, Seared, with Soy
     Broth and, 69
SQUASH
   Butternut, Orzo Risotto with Bacon and, 121
   Yellow, and Smoked-Mozzarella Pizzettes,
     Grilled, 130, 130
STEAK(S)
   Filet Mignon with Mustard Sauce,
     62, 62
   Grilled, Salad with Pickle-Pepper
     Vinaigrette, 44, 45
   grilling time, 84
   Rib-Eye, Grilled, on Sautéed Onions and
     Garlic Croûtes with Curry Oil, 18, 19
   Rib-Eye, with Stilton Sauce, 81, 81
   Skirt, Ancho-Chile, Pan-Seared, 66
   Strip, Grilled, with Olive-Oregano Relish,
     77, 78
STEW, Chicken and Chickpea, Saffron, 26, 27
STILTON
   Endive, and Bacon Salad, 156, 157
   Sauce, Rib-Eye Steak with, 81, 81
STIR-FRY(IED)
   Chicken, with Shiitakes, Snow Peas, and Pea
     Shoots, 65
   Pork with Broccoli and Ginger, Spicy, 70

Tuna "Chop Chop" Salad, *52*, 53
STRAWBERRY Balsamic Sauce, 189
STRIP STEAKS, Grilled, with Olive-Oregano
    Relish, 77, 78
SUCCOTASH, 138
SUGAR SNAP PEA(S)
    and Couscous Salad with Pistachios, 128
    Malfada with Smoked Salmon and, 124
    Quinoa with Tarragon and, 148
    and Smoked Chicken Salad with Mint,
        42, 43
SWEET POTATO(ES)
    Chips with Lime Salt, *169*, 170
    Sesame-Soy, 138
SWISS CHEESE with Walnuts and Mustard, *170*,
    170

T

TACOS, Cod, Fried, 70
TARRAGON
    Pea Soup with, Chilled, 97
    Quinoa with Sugar Snap Peas and, 148
TARTS, Kiwifruit Shortbread, 184, *185*
TERIYAKI Turkey Cutlets, Grilled, 83
THAI Ground-Pork Salad with Mint and Cilantro,
    48, 49
THOUSAND ISLAND DRESSING, Low-Fat, *162*,
    163
TOASTS
    Bruschetta with White Beans and Walnuts,
        172, 172
    Croûtes, Garlic, Grilled Rib-Eye Steaks on
        Sautéed Onions and, with Curry Oil, *18*, 19
    Pita, Cumin, Crab Canapés on, Light, 174
    Pita, Fennel, 173
TOMATILLO
    Salsa, Celery, *86*, 87
    Sauce, Lemon, Campanelle with, 124
TOMATO(ES)
    Charred, Salsa, Chipotle, Mango and,
        88, 88
    Cherry, and Lamb Kebabs, Grilled, with
        Guacamole, 78
    Chicken Roasted with Potatoes, Olives and,
        30, 31
    Gazpacho with Parsley Pesto, Quick, 100
    Lentil Soup with Spinach and, 95
    Pizza Margherita, 131
    Pizza, White Bean, Goat Cheese and, 132
    with Salsa Verde, 141
    Sauce, -Basil Clam, Linguine with,
        118, 119
TORTELLINI with Baby Spinach and Garlic, 123

TORTILLA(S). *See also* Quesadillas
    Rolls, Turkey and Black-Bean Salsa,
        108, 108
    Tacos, Cod, Fried, 70
TUNA
    "Chop Chop" Salad, Stir-Fried, *52*, 53
    with Greek Salad, *40*, 41
    Pasta Salad, Warm, with Baby Spinach and,
        54, 55
    Steaks, Seared, with Radish Sprouts and Soy
        Broth, 69
TURKEY
    and Black-Bean Salsa Tortilla Rolls, *108*, 108
    Burgers, Herbed, 113
    Club Sandwiches, -Watercress, *109*, 109
    Cutlets Teriyaki, Grilled, 83
    in Jade, Chinese, *50*, 51
    Sausage, Orecchiette with Marinara Sauce
        and, 128
    Smoked, Mango and Chipotle Mayo Wraps,
        107
TURNIPS, Mashed, 143

V

VEAL Scallopini with Mushrooms and Marsala, 73
VEGETABLE(S). *See also* names of vegetables
    and Brown Rice Salad, Crunchy, 152, *153*
    Chicken Legs, Roasted, with Arugula and, *14*,
        15
    Couscous, 75
    Soup, Barley, 101
    Succotash, 138
VINAIGRETTE
    Everyday, 163
    Ginger-Miso, 166
    Hazelnut, Warm, Dandelion Salad with, *155*,
        156
    Pickle-Pepper, Grilled Steak Salad with, *44*,
        45
    Sherry-Mustard, Arugula-Parsley Salad with
        Chickpeas, Pickles, and, *158*, 158
    Soy-Sesame, 166

W

WALNUT(S)
    Bruschetta with White Beans and, *172*, 172
    Chicory Salad with Goat Cheese and, 161
    and Feta Quesadillas with Apple-Fig Salsa,
        114, *115*
    Red Pepper Dip with, *170*, 171
    Swiss Cheese with Mustard and, *170*, 170

WATERCRESS
    and Chicken Salad, Crispy Asian, *36*, 37
    Sesame, and Cucumber Salad, 156
    Turkey Club Sandwiches, *109*, 109
WATERMELON, Cantaloupe, and Red Pepper
    Salsa, *86*, 87
WHITE BEAN(S). *See* Bean(s)
WON TON Strips, Crispy, Berry Compote with
    Vanilla Ice Cream and, 179
WRAPS
    Hummus, Carrot, and Cucumber Lavash, 110
    Turkey, Smoked, Mango and Chipotle Mayo,
      107

Y

YELLOW SQUASH, and Smoked-Mozzarella
    Pizzettes, Grilled, *130*, 130
YOGURT
    Chipotle Sauce with Cumin, 89
    Dip, Lemon-, Caramelized Figs with, 180
    Raita, Mango, Red Snapper, Grilled Indian-
      Spiced Whole, with, 80
    Sauce, Lamb Chops, Lemon-Garlic, with, 74

Z

ZUCCHINI
    Ribbons, Chive, 141
    Soup, Herb, Chilled, 96

TABLE SETTING
acknowledgments

Any items in the photographs not credited are privately owned.

FRONTMATTER

Dog with Slipper (page 1): *Foulard printed velvet slippers—Stubbs & Wooton, (212) 249-5200.*
Saffron Chicken and Chickpea Stew; Fennel Pita Toast (page 6): See credits below for "One-Dish Dinners"
A New Chef's Salad (page 7): See credits below for "Salads for Dinner."

ONE-DISH DINNERS

Roasted Chicken Legs with Vegetables and Arugula (page 14): *Wüsthof steak knife (from a set of 4)—Broadway Panhandler, (212) 966-3434.*
Roasted Mussels with Almonds and Garlic (page 16): *"Bistro Menu" ceramic dinner plates and soup bowls; "Gingham Stripe" cotton kitchen towels—Williams-Sonoma, (800) 840-2591.*
Grilled Rib-Eye Steaks on Sautéed Onions and Garlic Croûtes with Curry Oil (page 18): *Plates, tablecloth, and napkins—Williams-Sonoma, (800) 840-2591. "Mundial" steak knife (from a set of 4)—Broadway Panhandler, (212) 966-3434. French nineteenth-century bentwood bistro chair—Howard Kaplan Antiques, (212) 674-1000.*
Shrimp and Fennel Risotto (page 20): *"Dana" plates and bowls by Barbara Eigen; "Chop" silver-plate flatware—Pottery Barn, (800) 840-2843.*
Saffron Chicken and Chickpea Stew; Fennel Pita Toast (page 26): *"Alexa" earthenware bowl—for stores call Eigen Arts, Inc., (201) 798-7310. Iron-handled flatware—Tuscan Square, (212) 977-7777. Linen tablecloth—William-Wayne & Co., (212) 288-9243.*

SALADS FOR DINNER

A New Chef's Salad (page 34): *Ceramic bowl—Williams-Sonoma, (800) 840-2951. "Early English" sterling serving fork and spoon—James Robinson, (212) 752-6166.*
Crispy Asian Chicken and Watercress Salad (page 36): *"Grid" porcelain plates—for stores call Calvin Klein, (800) 294-7978. "Oval" stainless steel flatware by Boda Nova—Fillamento, (415) 931-2224. "Ambronay Paon" silk and rayon fabric and "Tyrol Pastel" napkin available through decorator—Clarence House, (212) 752-2890.*
Smoked Chicken and Sugar Snap Pea Salad with Mint (page 42): *"Twist Alea" faience dinner plate—Villeroy & Boch Creations, (212) 535-2500.*
Grilled Steak Salad with Pickle-Pepper Vinaigrette (page 44): *"Almost Round" ceramic dinner plates; lantern—Crate & Barrel, (800) 996-9960. "Claridge" wood-handled flatware—for stores call Mariposa, (800) 788-1304. Chair—Newel Art Galleries, (212) 758-1970.*
Shrimp Cocktail Exotique (page 46): *Ceramic dinner plate by Sasaki—for stores call (212) 686-7440.*
Thai Ground-Pork Salad with Mint and Cilantro (page 48): *Jade bowl—Global Table, (212) 431-5839. Woven-grass and wood tray—Jamson Whyte, (212) 965-9405. Tiger bamboo place mats—Ad Hoc Softwares, (212) 925-2652.*
Chinese Turkey in Jade (page 50): *Plates and flatware—Banana Republic, (888) 906-2800.*
Stir-Fried Tuna "Chop Chop" Salad (page 52): *"Trifid" hand-forged sterling knife and forks; "Round English" hand-forged sterling knife and fork —James Robinson, (212) 752-6166.*

QUICK STOVE-TOP DISHES

Cornmeal-Crusted Chicken with Toasted Corn Salsa (page 57): *"À la Ferme" porcelain plates—Villeroy & Boch Creation, (212) 535-2500. French Acrylic flatware by Sabre—Marel Gifts, (800) 261-3501.*
Sautéed Sea Scallops with Mustard Sauce (page 61, top): *Ceramic plates by Cyclamen from the L·S Collection, (212) 334-1194.*
Pan-Seared Halibut with Salsa Verde (page 61, bottom): *Ceramic plates—for stores call Vietri, (800) 277-5933.*
Filet Mignon with Mustard Sauce (page 62, top): *"Hunslet Collection" creamware dinner plate by Hartley Greens & Co.—Erika Reade, Ltd., (404) 233-3857. "Brummell" crystal wineglass—Baccarat, (800) 777-0100. "Luna" porcelain dessert/salad plates and "York" stainless-steel flatware—for stores call Calvin Klein, (800) 294-7978. Linen placemats and napkins—ABH Designs, (212) 688-3764.*

SEARED SEA BASS WITH FRESH HERBS AND LEMON (PAGE 62, BOTTOM): "Velvet Stripe" linen napkin with velvet trim by Angel Zimick—Barneys New York, (212) 826-8900.

PAN-ROASTED CHICKEN WITH ORANGES, ROSEMARY, AND ALMONDS (PAGE 63): Dinner plate—Bridge Kitchenware, (800) 274-3435 or (212) 688-4220.

SEARED SESAME SCALLOPS; PEA AND MINT COUSCOUS (PAGE 71): "Hudson Bone" flatware—for stores call Calvin Klein, (800) 294-7978.

SMOKED SALMON FRITTATA WITH GOAT CHEESE (PAGE 74): Earthenware dinner and salad plates by Calvin Tsao—for stores call Nan Swid Design, (800) 808-7943.

QUICK GRILLS

RIB-EYE STEAK WITH STILTON SAUCE (PAGE 81, BOTTOM): "Cléopâtre" porcelain dinner plate—Bernardaud, (212) 371-4300.

TOMATILLO CELERY SALSA; SPICY PINEAPPLE, APRICOT, AND JÍCAMA SALSA; WATERMELON, CANTALOUPE, AND RED PEPPER SALSA (PAGE 86): Handwoven wool rebozo and handwoven cotton napkin—Pan American Phoenix, (212) 570-0300.

PORK CHOP WITH SAVORY DRIED CRANBERRY SAUCE (PAGE 88, LEFT): "Acadia Colors" stoneware dinner plate—Pfaltzgraff Co., (800) 999-2811.

CHARRED TOMATO, CHIPOTLE, AND MANGO SALSA (PAGE 88, RIGHT): See credits above for Tomatillo Celery Salsa.

QUICK SOUPS

MUSHROOM AND LEEK SOUP (PAGE 91): "Velvet Stripe" linen napkin with velvet trim by Angel Zimick—Barneys New York, (212) 826-8900.

HOW TO CHILL SOUPS (PAGE 96): "Craftworks" ceramic plates by Lindt Stymeist—ABC Carpet & Home, (212) 473-3000. PN "Carre" French hand-molded terra-cotta tiles (in Rouge)—Country Floors, (212) 627-8300.

RED LENTIL AND CARROT SOUP (PAGE 101): French nineteenth century faience soup bowl—Country Loft Antiques, (203) 266-4500.

QUICK SANDWICHES AND BURGERS

CURRIED CHICKEN AND MANGO SANDWICH (PAGE 103):

"Tsao Matte" luncheon and buffet plates by Calvin Tsao—for stores call Nan Swid Design, (800) 808-7943.

CRAB MELT SANDWICH (PAGE 105, TOP): "Topkapi" porcelain plates by Raynaud—Neiman Marcus, (800) 937-9146.

GUACAMOLE CHEESEBURGER (PAGE 113): "Les Marquises" Limoges salad plate and cotton napkin by Souleiado—Pierre Deux, (212) 570-9343.

RIPE OLIVE AND AVOCADO QUESADILLAS (PAGE 115, BOTTOM): "Natural Ware" service plate—for stores call Calvin Klein, (800) 294-7978. Napkin (background)—for stores call Dransfield & Ross, (212) 741-7278.

QUICK PASTAS AND PIZZAS

PASTA "RAGS" WITH A THOUSAND HERBS (PAGE 117): Ceramic soup bowl and dinner plate by Cassis; Italian pewter flatware—Zona, (212) 925-6750.

LINGUINE WITH TOMATO-BASIL CLAM SAUCE (PAGE 118): "Rushing Tide" glass bowl—for stores call Izabel Lam, (718) 797-3983. "Ripple" glass plate—for stores call Annieglass, (800) 347-6133.

PASTA WITH MUSSELS, ROASTED RED PEPPERS, AND BROCCOLI RABE (PAGE 126): Bowl—Bridge Kitchenware, (800) 274-3435 or (212) 688-4220.

QUICK VEGETABLES

BROILED LEEKS WITH BUTTERED BREAD CRUMBS (PAGE 135): "Bistro Menu" ceramic dinner plate; "Gingham Stripe" cotton kitchen towels—Williams-Sonoma, (800) 840-2591.

HERBED POTATO SALAD (PAGE 139, TOP): "Sophia" handmade porcelain bowl by Theresa W. Chang Ceramics—Shi, (212) 334-4330.

MOROCCAN SPICY CARROTS (PAGE 139, BOTTOM): "Ellipse" ceramic bowls—Pottery Barn, (800) 840-2843. Vintage cotton kitchen towel—Paula Rubenstein, (212) 966-8954.

QUICK GRAINS

CRUNCHY VEGETABLE AND BROWN RICE SALAD (PAGE 153): "Tellus" faience charger by Source Perrier; "Montpellier" pewter flatware; wood-and-iron bench by Source Perrier—Pierre Deux, (212) 570-9343. Travertine chiaro tiles—Country Floors, (212) 627-8300.

QUICK GREEN SALADS

DANDELION SALAD WITH WARM HAZELNUT VINAIGRETTE (PAGE 155): *Lavender glass plate by Pinkwater—Bergdorf Goodman, (212) 753-7300.*

ARUGULA-PARSLEY SALAD WITH CHICKPEAS, PICKLES, AND SHERRY-MUSTARD VINAIGRETTE (PAGE 158, TOP): *"Trifid" sterling knife and forks; "Round English" sterling knife and fork —James Robinson, (212) 752-6166.*

SESAME SPINACH AND BEET SALAD (PAGE 158, BOTTOM): *"Almost Round" ceramic dinner plates—Crate & Barrel (800) 996-9960.*

LOW-FAT BACON MUSTARD DRESSING; LOW-FAT HERBED RANCH DRESSING; LOW-FAT THOUSAND ISLAND DRESSING; LOW-FAT CHIPOTLE CHUTNEY DRESSING (PAGE 162): *Cruets— Bridge Kitchenware, (800) 274-3435 or (212) 688-4220.*

QUICK SNACKS

CHICKPEA, GARLIC, AND PARSLEY DIP; RED PEPPER DIP WITH WALNUTS; CREAMY CLAM DIP (PAGE 170, BOTTOM): *Platinum-glazed porcelain dishes—Gordon Foster, (212) 744-4922.*

SUN-DRIED TOMATO AND ROASTED RED PEPPER DIP (PAGE 174): *Handmade ceramic bowl and platter by Barbara Eigen—Dean & Deluca, Inc., (800) 999-0306.*

QUICK DESSERTS

COFFEE SOUFFLÉS WITH MOCHA SAUCE (PAGES 177 AND 178): *"Luna" porcelain dessert/salad plates and "York" stainless-steel flatware—for stores call Calvin Klein, (800) 294-7978. Linen placemats and napkins—ABH Designs, (212) 688-3764. Porcelain soufflé dishes—Bridge Kitchenware, (800) 274-3435 or (212) 688-4220.*

NECTARINES, PLUMS, AND BLUEBERRIES IN LEMONY GINGER ANISE SYRUP; CHOCOLATE CHUNK COOKIES WITH PECANS, DRIED APRICOTS, AND TART CHERRIES (PAGE 182): *"Dalli" crystal bowl—Rogaska, (212) 980-6200. Bandana—Paula Rubenstein, (212) 966-8954.*

KIWIFRUIT SHORTBREAD TART (PAGE 185, TOP): *"Grid" porcelain plate—for stores call Calvin Klein, (800) 294-7978. "Oval" stainless steel flatware by Boda Nova—Fillamento, (415) 931-2224. "Ambronay Paon" silk and rayon fabric available through decorator—Clarence House, (212) 752-2890.*

CREDITS

PHOTOGRAPHY

The following photographers have generously given permission to reprint their photographs. Some of these photos have previously appeared in *Gourmet* magazine.

Quentin Bacon
FILET MIGNON WITH MUSTARD SAUCE; BROCCOLI RABE; CRISP POTATO GALETTE (PAGE 62, TOP). *Copyright © 1999.* COFFEE SOUFFLÉS WITH MOCHA SAUCE (PAGES 177 AND 178). *Copyright © 1999.*

Stuart Haygarth
DINNER PLATE CLOCK (12, TOP). *Copyright © 2000.*

Alan Richardson
CORNED BEEF HASH (PAGE 22). *Copyright © 1999.* SHRIMP AND CORN WITH BASIL (PAGE 28). *Copyright © 1999.* PAN-ROASTED SALMON WITH GINGER AND CURRY; PICKLED CUCUMBER AND CABBAGE (PAGE 59). *Copyright © 1999.* PORK CHOPS WITH CORIANDER-CUMIN SPICE RUB; CREAMY PARMESAN POLENTA (PAGE 64). *Copyright © 1999.* BORSCHT (PAGE 92). *Copyright © 2000.* WARM GOAT CHEESE, BEET, AND ARUGULA SANDWICHES (PAGE 105, BOTTOM). *Copyright © 1999.* HERBED JASMINE RICE (PAGE 147). *Copyright © 1999.* ENDIVE, STILTON, AND BACON SALAD (PAGE 157). *Copyright © 1999.* BROILED APPLES WITH MAPLE CALVADOS SAUCE (PAGE 181). *Copyright © 1999.*

Ellen Silverman
FRONTISPIECE (PAGE 2). *Copyright © 1999.*

RECIPES

Grateful acknowledgment is made to the following contributors for permission to reprint recipes previously published in *Gourmet* magazine.

Jody Adams (Rialto, Cambridge, MA)
PASTA WITH MUSSELS, ROASTED RED PEPPERS, AND BROCCOLI RABE (PAGE 127). *Copyright © 1996.*

Ed Brown
STIR-FRIED TUNA "CHOP CHOP" SALAD (PAGE 52). *Copyright © 1998.* ARUGULA-PARSLEY SALAD WITH CHICKPEAS, PICKLES, AND SHERRY-MUSTARD VINAIGRETTE (PAGE 158). *Copyright © 1998.*

Janie Hibler
GRILLED SALMON STEAKS WITH GINGER BUTTER (PAGE 80). *Copyright © 1997.*

Lakeview Inn, New Preston, CT
SMOKED SALMON FRITTATA WITH GOAT CHEESE (PAGE 74). *Copyright © 1999.*

Michael Lomonaco
PAN-ROASTED CHICKEN WITH ORANGES, ROSEMARY, AND ALMONDS (PAGE 63). *Copyright © 1996.*

Laura M. Ortega
BROILED CHICKEN AND ROASTED PEPPER SANDWICHES (PAGE 109). *Copyright © 1999.*

Elizabeth Perez
PLANTAIN SOUP (PAGE 95). *Copyright © 1998.*

James Peterson
MOROCCAN SPICY CARROTS (PAGE 139). *Copyright © 1998.*

Michele Scicolone
PASTA "RAGS" WITH A THOUSAND HERBS (PAGE 119). *Copyright © 1996.*

Ellen Shriver
GREEN NOODLES WITH GARLIC (PAGE 123). *Copyright © 1999.*

Zanne Early Stewart
SHRIMP COCKTAIL EXOTIQUE (PAGE 47). *Copyright © 1996.* RIB-EYE STEAK WITH STILTON SAUCE (PAGE 81). *Copyright © 1993.* CRAB MELT SANDWICHES, (PAGE 104). *Copyright © 1997.* GUACAMOLE CHEESEBURGERS (PAGE 113). *Copyright © 1992.*

recipe key
A Guide to Using *Gourmet*'s Recipes

•**Measure liquids** in glass or clear plastic liquid-measuring cups; **dry ingredients** in nesting dry-measuring cups (usually made of metal or plastic) that can be leveled off with a knife.

•**Measure flour** by spooning (not scooping) it into a dry-measuring cup and leveling off with a knife without tapping or shaking cup.

•Do not **sift flour** unless specified in recipe. If sifted flour is called for, sift flour before measuring. (Many brands say "presifted" on the label; disregard this.)

•When we call for a **shallow baking pan**, we mean an old-fashioned jelly-roll or 4-sided cookie pan.

•**Measure skillets** and **baking pans** across the top, not across the bottom.

•Use light-colored **metal pans** for baking unless otherwise specified. If using dark metal pans, including nonstick, your baked goods will likely brown more and the cooking times may be shorter.

•Wash and dry all **produce** before using.

•Before prepping fresh **herbs or greens**, remove the leaves or fronds from the stems—the exception is cilantro, which has tender stems.

•Pack fresh **herbs and greens** before measuring.

•Black **pepper** in recipes is always freshly ground.

•Wear protective gloves when handling **chiles**.

•Grate **cheeses** just before using.

•To **zest** citrus fruits, remove the colored part of the rind only (avoid the bitter white pith). For strips, use a vegetable peeler. For grated zest, use the smallest teardrop-shaped holes or the tiny sharp ones on a four-sided grater.

•**Toast spices** in a dry heavy skillet over moderate heat, stirring, until fragrant and a shade or two darker. Toast nuts in a shallow baking pan in a 350°F oven until golden, 5 to 10 minutes. **Toast seeds** either way.

•**To peel** a tomato, first cut an X in the end opposite the stem and immerse in boiling water 10 seconds. Transfer it to ice water and then peel.